You'll Neve
A True Story abou

by Debbie Singh

First published in 2006 by
Maverick House Publishers,
Main Street,
Dunshaughlin,
Co. Meath,
Ireland.
info@maverickhouse.com
http://www.maverickhouse.com

ISBN: 1-905379-10-2
978-1-905379-10-1

5 4 3 2 1

Printed by Nørhaven Paperback, Denmark.

The paper used in this book comes from wood pulp of managed forests. For every tree felled at least one tree is planted, thereby renewing natural resources.

DEDICATION

To Sister Joan; a woman's woman whose empathy and sense of social justice for the sick and poor in Bangkok inspired me to reach out to others. Thank you. You gave me a priceless gift.

ACKNOWLEDGEMENTS

Setting out on this journey seven years ago, I could never have imagined the dizzy highs and the debilitating lows I have experienced, and I would like to thank all of those people who helped me through this time.

Firstly, I could never have achieved a thing without the unconditional love and support of my husband Richard. He stood by me through thick and thin, putting up with my emotional roller-coaster ride and giving me the freedom to travel to Thailand ten times. I promise I'll never moan again when you want to go fishing!

Our boys Sean, Michael, Kieran and Jason had it tough at times, especially when we moved house to keep financing 'Mum's crusade for John'—thanks for being the best kids in the world.

Growing up in Liverpool and coming from a large working-class family, Mum and Dad brought us up to always put family first, so Mum and Dad, thank you for that gift, and for your love and financial support. Thanks too to our Tricia, who was always there for me, as were my brothers Kevin, Pat and Barry.

Most of the time I was so consumed by my crusade for John that I lost touch with friends and family. To those who stood by me and never judged me, I thank you for that.

Thanks to Julie Dabala, a special lady who reached out and touched our lives, and to Keith who was always there to put me back together.

I have journeyed to a part of the world I never thought I'd see, experiencing the good and bad of human nature, teaching me valuable lessons I'll carry with me for the rest of my life. My heartfelt thanks go to Sister Joan Evans for sharing her world with me in Bangkok, and opening my eyes.

Details of Sister Joan's wonderful work can be found at www.sisterjoan.info

Yvonne Ziegler, whose never-ending love and support still continues today; you are priceless. Although at times I had a rocky relationship with Australian Embassy staff, I would like to say a big thank you to Warren MacIlwain, Kraisorn, Johnson and Robin Hamilton-Coates. You were my security blanket in Bangkok.

Thanks to Dr John Lerwitworapong at Klong Prem hospital, for opening doors for me. Thanks also to Khun Somphon, Khun Thitiporn and Pornpitsami from Foreign Affairs in Klong Prem, for always welcoming me with open arms.

The beautiful Nat and the cranky old so-and-so Norman—without their help, Jason would not be with us today. I'm indebted to you forever.

Thanks to John Kealy for all his wonderful help.

A big thank you to Mandy Godfry at Thai Airways, who took my call five years ago begging for excess baggage allowance. Hundreds of kilos, and lots of love and support later, you are a true mate who has always been there.

There are many people who I have not personally met, but without whom life would have been unbearable at times. To Diane and the kids in Sydney, you are unsung heroes who I love and respect. To Lynn, who was banging on doors for the Transfer Treaty to be ratified long before I came on the scene. You gave me strength and pushed me to open doors. Thank you.

To all the families of prisoners, in Thailand or anywhere in the world, my heart goes out to you; don't give up.

Thanks also to Bill and Pauline Johnson, who bought all the Liverpool FC gear I had, and my mate in Liverpool, Pat Miles, as well as her son John, who played for Liverpool in 2001, and the Fletcher family. Thanks to Liverpool FC and the Liverpool FC shareholders in Australia for their generous financial donations to our fundraising for Sister Joan.

And thanks to my family in Liverpool for their ongoing support and for taking the time to visit Trevor when they were on holiday in Bangkok.

Politics played a major role in this journey, and bureaucracy almost sent me loopy. Thank God for Chris Hodges at the Federal Attorney General's department. I know you will not like this bouquet but you saved me from despair many times.

Thanks to Kerin Lenard for your professionalism and humility.

Malcolm Penn here in Perth, thank you for putting up with my nagging phone calls and e-mails. And of course thanks to Brian Pontifax from the Justice Minister's office; you got us over the line. Cheers.

The journey continues to this day, so thank you to the amazing Trevor Lund, my mentor and at times psychiatrist. Thanks too to Martin, Bob, Alan, Holly, Debbie, Jane, Jagnathan, Peter and all the others who trusted in me and are still awaiting freedom.

A special thank you to Dr Wendy Were and Kath Mallott, who made me believe I had a story worth telling. Wendy, you inspired me from day one and without your dedication and encouragement I would have given up long ago.

Thanks to all at Maverick House Publishers; especially Adam, for having the patience of a saint.

— CHAPTER ONE —

One thing is for sure; you can never know from one day to the next what life has in store for you. Seven years ago, when I was merrily juggling a business, a household and a family, I would never have dreamed that in the coming years I'd be on the telephone discussing foreign affairs with the Australian Prime Minister, John Howard, or debating on-air with one of his key ministers, Alexander Downer. I never would have pictured myself comfortably sitting down to breakfast with the Governor of that infamous prison, the 'Bangkok Hilton', while outside 15 prison inmates ran a marathon that I had helped organise in order to raise money for disadvantaged children in the Bangkok slums. I never could have imagined that I would do many of the things that I've done, and lived through the incredible events that now form my memories. So many people have told me that my story is unbelievable. If I hadn't lived it, I think I would agree with them.

But what *is* unbelievable, really, is the capacity of humanity to treat strangers with such extremes—in the last seven years, I think I've witnessed the worst and the best of human behaviour, from utter contempt and degradation, to an awe-inspiring capacity for love, coupled with a genuine desire to make the world a better place for everyone. My journey has been harrowing at times, desperate at others, and sadly doesn't have the happy ending for which I had hoped. Still, I don't think there's much that I would have done differently, and though the ending is not what I first wanted to achieve, it has brought a lot more to my life than I could possibly have imagined.

* * *

I grew up in Liverpool, England, in a wonderfully loving family. I was the youngest of four children in the Doran household, my mother having had three boys before I was born. Kevin and Daniel were twins, but sadly Daniel died in infancy. Pat was born a year later, before I came along six years later; the only girl and the youngest member of the family. That was until the 1970s when my mother became increasingly interested in the idea of fostering. My older brothers were flying the coop —leaving home and getting married—and I don't think Mum could bear the thought of an 'empty nest'. My father was largely unaware that my mother had begun making enquiries to the Merseyside Social Services about fostering. I was privy to this secret and was so excited at the thought of having younger brothers or sisters. I was always hovering over her shoulder when she was on the phone to the agency, coaxing her on. I had been the youngest for long enough, I felt, and I didn't want to be the only one still at home either. We both began dropping hints and generally bringing up the subject whenever Dad was home from work, and it didn't take long before he cottoned on to what we were plotting and accepted with good-natured resignation that it was going to happen, with or without his blessing. I remember him saying something to the effect of; 'Do what you like—you always will anyway!' And so our family went through the screening process and within a few months, short-stay foster children who needed temporary accommodation, perhaps due to a parent being in hospital or because they were in pre-adoption proceedings, became part of our family.

John came into our family as a foster child when he was about seven years old, after a pretty rough start in life. He was a lost and very sad little boy; looking into his eyes you only saw sorrow. He had never had a father figure, and his mother, who had cerebral palsy, just wasn't capable of looking after him. The placement with us was not the first time John had been placed in care with other families. His mother had indicated that she could no longer cope with John, so his length of stay with us was always presumed to be long term. From the moment he entered our house, it was pretty obvious that this skinny little guy had been through a lot. When the social worker brought him to us, all he had with him were the clothes he wore, which were two sizes too small, a change of underwear, and a small box of broken toys. In anticipation of his arrival, Mum had already bought new clothes, toys and shoes, so within hours of joining our family, John's transformation began. He wolfed down every bit of food that was offered to him, and it was clear that he was undernourished.

It was impossible for our hearts not to go out to him, and our immediate and extended family quickly grew to love him as one of our own. And that is how I've always thought of him—as my brother. In my mind, the distinction between blood and foster relations seems ludicrous—if you grow up in the same house and share your lives together, the bonds are the same as blood ties. To this day it annoys the life out of me when people refer to him as somehow 'outside' of the family, simply because he is not my blood brother. For us, the sense of family was always very strong. We looked out for and supported each other, and always have. For me, this was no different when it came to John. He was one of us. Simple as that.

After John came to live with us, he and I quickly became very close, particularly as I was in my mid-teens and tended to spend more time with him, baby-sitting and collecting him from school. I was the only sibling he ever had, my older brothers having left home, and in a dramatic change that saw me go from a precocious, spoilt girl to a responsible older sister, I realised I was someone he would look up to. I was no longer the centre of the universe. I recognised that I had responsibilities, and that I needed to show John, who had been brought up in an emotionally barren environment, that he was loved. I was overwhelmed at the thought of him not having the stable loving home, with two loving parents, that I had, and I was determined to fill that gap. The bond between us grew strong as a result. It didn't take long before I felt as though he had always been a part of our family. I used to love babysitting and minding John when my parents went to the Dockers Club. We'd have great fun stuffing our faces with sweets in front of the Saturday night movie, and most of the time I'd let him stay up late, until we heard the taxi bringing Mum and Dad home and would have to dash up the stairs and hop into bed.

I loved John's dry sense of humour, which he had developed early on in life. But he would also try your patience. After years of telling us he was an Everton supporter, he finally confessed that he only said it to rub us up the wrong way. He was in fact, like all of us, a mad Liverpool fan.

From the very beginning though, John was a bit of a loner. While he was always a good laugh and we got along so well, he was a solitary soul who never shared much of himself with anybody and seemed happier keeping to himself. I guess he was used to being passed around and found it difficult to grow close to anyone for fear of losing them again. We did our best to make sure he always felt like he was one of us and that we weren't going to let him go it alone. As his older sister I made sure I was there for him, and in his way he responded in kind, as we grew as close as any brother and sister could. My parents took on another foster-child, Barry, a year later, and he too helped John feel like part of a family.

But John also didn't seem to have a defined sense of personal direction and wasn't driven or passionate about anything in particular. He was a quiet kind of person, but I got the sense that there were things in his life that only he knew about. At times, he seemed to be lost in his own world.

Life was fairly uneventful, until my two older brothers got married within two months of each other, and their families made the decision to move from Liverpool to Western Australia. Kevin emigrated in 1978 with Pat following him in 1980. It wasn't long before I had followed them for my first overseas trip, enjoying two working holidays so much that I too decided to move to Australia permanently. About one year after me, in 1985, my parents, wanting to be with their children and grandchildren, decided to make the big move too. They had by this time legally adopted both John and Barry, so the whole family was soon on the move to Australia. It was a wrench for them to leave behind their extended families in Liverpool, as well as their lifestyles. Dad had worked on the docks for 30 years and Mum had a good job in a finance company, but they took the plunge, and after spending some time in Sydney with Pat, they came to West Australia to join up with Kevin and I, settling in the north-eastern goldfields town of Leinster where my brothers and I were working. My parents found work easily; Dad in the mill and Mum in the canteen there, and John was given his first job, in the mining stores.

We all loved it, except for John, who didn't adjust to his new environment easily. He was a Liverpudlian teenager who had just left school, and had been transported from a northern English city to a small mining town in the outback of Australia, with a nickel mine and a population of 1,200. He may as well have been transplanted to the moon. Unsurprisingly, he didn't feel like he fitted in. It was not long before he took off from Leinster without letting any of us know of his plans. We assumed he had headed to the nearby town of Kalgoorlie, as there were few other places to go, and waited to hear from him, but after a few days of worrying and hoping he would come back, I went to the local police station and made some subtle enquiries to see if I could locate him. The desk sergeant was very helpful, and sure enough, within a couple of minutes our John's name popped up on the computer screen—it seemed John had recently been caught stealing a bar of chocolate at a supermarket in the south-west town of Albany.

We were disappointed in him, but relieved to know his whereabouts. About a week or so later, Mum and I made the eighteen-hour bus trip to find him, and arrived in Albany in the early evening. We checked into a motel, then went out on to the town streets and asked a few locals where the teenagers tended to hang out. We were pointed in the direction of the local bowling alley and we immediately headed there in a taxi. Would you believe; there was John, lounging around with a group of new-found friends, looking like he didn't have a care in the world? If he was surprised to see us, it didn't register on his face. The three of us went back to the motel and we managed to talk him into coming back home with us. He was a little sorry for himself, not least because in order to feed himself he had picked up some work mowing lawns, and had badly cut his hand as a result. The bandage was dirty and he looked like he'd been living rough. Little did we know that this wouldn't be the last rescue mission for our John.

We didn't stay in Leinster much longer after that as the mine was closing down, so we all moved on to Perth, and when John was about 18 he moved out of my parents' house. He didn't seem to settle anywhere after that. He spent some time living with me in Perth, working as a push bike courier for a while, and then took off for Sydney when he was about 19. From there, he just drifted along, keeping in contact every few months but generally keeping his own life private. We knew that he had worked in a Thai restaurant in Sydney and had become quite attached to the Thai community, particularly his Thai girlfriend, and had spent time in South-East Asia, but the communication was so sporadic that most of the time we weren't entirely sure where he was. It was anybody's guess really. He knew we were there for him if he needed us, that he would always have a loving, caring family to turn to, and so we were quite happy to let him find his own path and live his own life. It didn't really matter that we didn't know where he was, once he knew where we were, and that we would always be there for him.

I settled in well, and as the years passed I got married and started my own business. My husband Richard and I had twin boys, Michael and Kieran, and around the same time my business, a fashion boutique, got up and running. I was fully immersed in my life in Australia, with my own growing family, but I was also grateful to have my parents and brothers around for support if ever I needed it. It was a pity John didn't seem to be around much any more, but

I knew that the bond between us was strong enough to survive any distance and time.

* * *

I remember quite clearly the day my life changed forever. I was changing the window displays in my boutique when I received the phone call from my mother. Mum called to tell me that she had received a letter from John, which was surprising enough in itself as he had been out of contact for some time. Mum read the letter to me over the phone, and I was instantly in shock. I couldn't believe it:

Dear Mum,

Sorry it's taken me so long to write but I've been putting it off, until it got so long I didn't know how to begin.

I'm in prison. About ten months ago I lost my passport. When I reported it to the police they told me my name is not John, it's Loizos, who was wanted for using forged traveller's cheques.

At first I wasn't worried and just let the police get on with it, because I thought that it shouldn't take them long to work out that I'm John.

At first it was OK, the police finished the investigation, saw there was no evidence and released me, but other police were waiting at the gate and rearrested me for the same case. I thought it would get dismissed but the prosecutor saw I'd been there before so he decided to charge me. So far I've been fighting the charges, just asking them to find a small piece of evidence to say that I'm guilty but apparently over here you don't need evidence.

The next time I go to court is 25 February and after talking to my friend, he advises me to plead guilty because fighting a case over here you will probably be in prison longer if you plead guilty in the first place, whether you win or lose. So I thought I'd better write and let you know. Sorry if it's a bit of a shock but it was a bit of a shock for me… OH! By the way, you have another grandson named Christopher Jason Doran, so you can add that to your list.

I'll give you my address in case you want to write. But the main thing is I wanted to let you know where I was.

Lots of love,
John.

I stopped what I was doing, my head spinning, unable to take in what I had just been told. *What was he saying? What did this mean? Would we ever see him again?* The letter opened up a whole new world to us, sending my life in all sorts of directions, but it really told us nothing more than the bare facts, and at the time I had no idea how much it would affect my life. That he was in Thailand was not too much of a shock. But nothing could have prepared me for the contents of the rest of the letter. My brother was in a prison in Bangkok. And to make matters far worse, he had already been there for seven months! The letter was an extraordinary piece of writing and now years later when I think about it, or read it in the cold light of day, it still takes the wind out of me:

I hated myself for it, but as I listened to Mum reading the letter to me again, a feeling of *déjà vu* washed over me. I was angry with him. Although I was shocked and upset to hear of my brother's situation, this was not the first time John had been in strife in Thailand. A few years earlier he had overstayed his visa and had been detained at the Immigration Detention Centre. My parents had to send him AU$1,000 to pay his fine and return airfare. But this was a very different and far more serious state of affairs, and the events that unfolded over the next few weeks defy belief. Already we couldn't believe what he was telling us—and how he casually mentioned that he now had a son. There were so many questions we needed answers to, but we knew we weren't going to get them.

After hearing Mum's news and realising how much trouble John could be in, my first instinct was to get a plane and fly over to John, to see where my brother was being held and do something, anything, to get him out. But I had to be realistic. I had a family of my own, and a business to run, and I couldn't just up and leave. I also had to recognise that having been in prison for months already, it was going to be a slow process with no easy answers or quick fixes. I had to approach things sensibly, so I told Mum that I would call the Department of Foreign Affairs and Trade (DFAT) to see if they could shed some light on John's situation and advise us on what to do to help him. This phone call yielded some strange information: we discovered that John had actually refused DFAT the permission to contact us, which meant that the Department had been prevented from corresponding with us up until this point. I couldn't believe it. *What was John doing? Why didn't he want us to help?*

The story slowly emerged and gained some clarity. John, who was now twenty seven years old, had been arrested for traveller's cheque fraud. The practice of selling forged cheques is rife in Thailand, and at the time of his offence, John was broke and his Thai girlfriend was five months pregnant. He was about to start work selling milk to hotels but needed some money to tide him over. So in a Bangkok bar one night, when a stranger offered him some US traveller's cheques, he bought three forged cheques with the money he had left, went to the hotel lobby to cash them, and had been caught in the process. The hotel alerted the police, who took John into custody. The value of the cheques he had attempted to pass was approximately US$1,000. It angered me too that we were finding out the truth from a faceless government department, and not from my brother himself, who had made up a story about mistaken identity.

Soon after though, my anger subsided and I began to feel sorry for poor John. He had got himself in trouble and didn't know where to turn. Maybe he was too ashamed to tell us the full story of what he had done, and had only plucked up the courage to tell us where he was when it got to the stage that he had to tell somebody before it was too late—before he vanished into the prison system. Even then, it seemed, he couldn't come clean to us about what really happened, and he was facing into some serious trouble.

By the time we were contacted, John was still to make his final court appearance and DFAT were unsure what kind of sentence he could expect. After all, he had fallen foul of the Thai judicial system, which is renowned for long prison terms and harsh sentences. I nominated myself as John's next of kin, because I felt like I was the closest to him, but also because I couldn't bear the thought of my parents dealing with the stress and bureaucracy that I could see lay ahead for us.

Already I was finding it extremely frustrating keeping up to date with what was happening. My daily habit of phoning the DFAT resulted in me coming off the phone either really happy or in tears, depending on which faceless name spoke to me. I wasn't getting much sympathy from them. I kept calling the Australian Embassy in Bangkok too, but they kept referring me back to Canberra, which I thought was strange. Surely the Embassy would have dealt with similar situations in the past? The lack of information was driving me crazy.

During the next month, I stayed in regular contact with DFAT hoping for any news—they said they too were waiting to hear from the Australian Embassy in Bangkok, but the repeated message was that there was nothing they could do until John went to trial. I had somehow managed to get over the shock of my little brother being in a Bangkok prison, surrounded by murderers, drug dealers and rapists, for what was really only a petty crime, and I was doing my best to lull myself into a false sense of security, and preparing myself for the news of a six month sentence. As John had already spent nine months in the prison, I really didn't think it would be too long before I would be organising his plane ticket back to Australia.

The day after John's court appearance in March, I rang DFAT, steeling myself to hear the absolute worst—that John had been given a one year sentence in a Thai jail. After all, it was only a forged cheque for the equivalent of AU$1,000, so it couldn't have been that serious. As I held the receiver to my ear, helplessly hoping for the best possible outcome of John being cleared, the government officer began reading, word for word, the report sent by the Australian Embassy in Bangkok. But after she read it out, I was certain she had got it wrong. It had to be a mistake. Had to be. Because the words 'ten years' were reverberating in my ears, making the rest of the report a blur. It didn't matter whatever else was in that document. The bottom line was that John had been found guilty of the three charges against him and had been given a ten year prison sentence. I felt myself reeling, my head swimming with questions and worries, and I didn't know what to do.

I hung up the phone, stunned. As the enormity of it all overcame me, I burst into a torrent of tears and ran into the privacy of the back of my shop, sobbing uncontrollably, feeling as though I had just been given the news of the death of a loved one. What really got to me was the severity of the sentence. I just couldn't believe it. Ten years! My brother was being locked up in prison for ten years! If John had committed the same crime in Australia, he would probably have received a community service order. But because he had committed this crime in Thailand, not only was he in a prison cell, he was also being subjected to the extreme violence and horrific conditions commonplace in Thai prisons. I had to try hard not to imagine the worst, what might be happening to John at each moment, but at times it just overwhelmed me. My mind raced with impossible questions—how on earth could I break this news to my parents? How do you tell your Mum and Dad that their son will be spending the next ten years in the shocking conditions of a Thai prison? I'm ashamed to say that when that moment actually came and I had to confront them with the terrible news, I failed miserably.

I didn't want my parents to suffer any more than they had to, and I knew telling them the severity of his sentence in a third world prison would devastate them completely. John had already been dealt a short straw in life from an early age, and I knew Mum and Dad wanted to protect him any way they could.

Calling to their home was almost a daily ritual and the first thing they would ask was always, 'Any news about John?' This time, I walked straight to the kettle, turned it on, and tried to be as casual as I could as I told them I had just received a call about his sentence. I looked at their hopeful, caring faces, and I just couldn't do it. I could only bring myself to tell them that John had been given a two year sentence. I know I had no right to lie and it was wrong of me to do so, but at the time, I could only think about protecting them from the truth. Even then, the news was shocking and Mum reacted with an 'Oh my God', while Dad just stood there stunned, saying over and over, 'That can't be right, that can't be right. If it was here, he would have got a fine.' I can't imagine what they would have done if I'd told them the truth. I think they both would have had a heart attack. I ranted on about King's Pardons and Prisoner Exchange Treaties, hoping this would give them something positive to think about, but it wasn't until over a year later that they learned the real length of John's sentence.

The next few weeks were spent constantly calling DFAT in Canberra and writing to John, trying to obtain as much information as possible so we could plan what to do next, while keeping my parents informed of everything they needed to know. The main thing to find out was whether or not John could appeal his sentence. The weeks passed agonisingly slowly but eventually I received a letter from John letting us know that he had written to a lawyer. He had found the name on a list provided to him by the Australian Embassy, but the lawyer turned out to be a corporate lawyer and therefore had been unable to help him. This messing about had wasted crucial time and as a result of the incorrect information supplied by the Embassy, John's period of appeal had now expired. On reading his letter telling me what had happened, my fury grew as I tried to get my head around it. How could the Australian Embassy have been so negligent as to provide an out-of-date and inaccurate list to one of their nationals facing a ten year prison sentence? This effectively cost him the chance to appeal. This was appalling, and I was enraged by the complacency of the Embassy staff and the casual way that lives were being played with. Foreign prisoners didn't seem to rate highly on the list of Embassy priorities; if anything, they seemed to be an annoying thorn in the side of Embassy staff. I wanted to meet them face to face and ask them why they had given John an out-of-date list. (An updated list was promptly made up after I talked to them). I was still living in denial to some extent, still waiting for a phonecall from DFAT or the Bangkok Embassy telling me it was all a mistake and John was on his way home. But that call never came, and after a while, I realised it never would. I was sick with worry.

I had heard stories and seen programmes on TV about the conditions in Thai prisons before, and over the next few years my worst fears would be confirmed as I witnessed them for myself. I had seen documentaries that showed them as generally overcrowded, with the heat inside just overwhelming. The thick stench of human bodies packed together in cramped and humid conditions seemed nauseating. The accounts I heard were horrifying: inmates were often locked up for sixteen hours a day. There was no Western food at all, access to clean water difficult, soap was not provided and diseases spread quickly. At this point, John had already spent over one year in the Bumbud Remand Prison in Thailand. It must have been such a traumatic experience; I remember in one of those rare moments when John opened up and talked about some of the things he endured whilst in prison, he told me that one of his strongest, most vivid memories from Bumbud was witnessing a Thai prisoner being beaten to death by his fellow inmates, apparently for nothing more than a difference of opinion. The guards did nothing to stop it.

Mum and I regularly wrote letters and sent parcels to Bumbud, and although John regularly wrote back now that he had broken the terrible news, he never went into much detail about how he felt or what was happening in his life. At this stage there was little we could do except just try to be there for him and provide him with food, and more importantly, emotional and financial support. But it was hard to be there for him when we were so far away, and so removed from what he was going through. The prison also had a bad record for delivering parcels to the inmates, so we were never sure if our packages were getting through. A day never went by without me thinking of my brother's horrendous situation, and imagining what he was doing, how he was coping, and what he was being subjected to. Crying myself to sleep soon became a nightly ritual. I felt so helpless and I desperately wanted to visit John in Thailand to see firsthand how he was, but I was operating a full-time business and looking after my three young boys, with a husband working away in the mines, so it just seemed impossible.

For me, 1998 was a lost year. Months passed with no development in John's situation. The only positive moment I can remember was when John was moved to Klong Prem prison, next door to Bumbud, where the conditions were slightly better and it was said that the guards treated the inmates more humanely. Still, it's all relative—Klong Prem is the official name for the notorious 'Bangkok Hilton', and has a reputation for being one of the world's toughest prisons. Overcrowding, violence and corruption are commonplace and while John's situation may have improved, it was still a terrible place; a place nobody would want their little brother to be.

— CHAPTER TWO —

Life carried on at home, almost as usual, but my awareness of John's circumstances was like a constant humming, the steady beating of a muffled drum, always present in the background. Reality truly set in when one day in 1999, after he had spent almost two years in prison, I received a letter from DFAT advising me that a prison contact visit with John would be possible in August of that year. If I wanted to take advantage of this rare opportunity to see John in person, I was told that I'd need to give them plenty of notice so that they could apply to the Thai Corrections Department for permission and organise the visit.

Although visits to Klong Prem inmates are permitted during the week, contact is usually limited to shouting through sets of bars and mesh, along with all the other visitors simultaneously trying to have a conversation. A contact visit where you can sit down together, and touch, and share food is restricted to a once-yearly privilege for all inmates, whether Thai or foreigners. During the annual contact visit period, two one-hour visits are allowed to take place over a five day period.

It didn't take much for me to make up my mind about what I had to do. After languishing helplessly for over a year while my brother lived in what he consistently described as a 'hellhole', I just couldn't miss the chance to have the contact visit, to see him face to face, to hug him and reassure myself that he was surviving despite everything. Going to Bangkok and directly dealing with the authorities there had to be a better way of helping our John, especially when nothing seemed to come of anything I was doing in Perth. What good was I doing phoning the DFAT all the time anyway? What could they do? I felt like I was too far removed from his situation, both physically and emotionally. When my husband called home from the mines that night, I shared my plan with him, knowing deep down that he would support me. Sure enough, understanding how important this trip was to me, Richard told me to go ahead and book my flight, and that we would manage to find the money somehow.

And so I began to put plans in place to travel to Thailand. I had never travelled to South-East Asia before and it was a little daunting. I scoured maps of Bangkok to find a hotel close to the prison, as I had heard about the terrible traffic and didn't want to waste time and money getting stuck in traffic jams. I found the Sofitel Central Plaza, about eight kilometres from Klong Prem. Having never been to Thailand, and feeling very nervous about travelling there alone, it was also important for me to feel safe. A four star hotel, coupled with a gut feeling that I'd be secure there, made that decision easy, and I booked my room.

I constantly talked to DFAT in Canberra and I had also contacted Roy Clogston, who at that time was the Australian Consul in Bangkok. Roy was very pleasant; I had spoken to him on the telephone when liaising with DFAT staff and the Australian Embassy, who were sorting out all the red tape associated with my contact visit for the Thai Corrections Department. I felt confident that I was in good hands.

Although I was anxious about the trip, I was also incredibly excited about the prospect of seeing my brother for the first time in so long, regardless of the circumstances. The idea that I could bring in things to him was thrilling, and I asked John what he needed, and what I was allowed to bring into the prison. He sent me an aerogramme with a list of requests, and topping it was Cherry Ripe chocolate bars, followed by Weetabix cereal, Vegemite, curry powder, mustard, cheese, Twisties, science fiction books, round-neck T-shirts and blue shorts with pockets. I was also told that we could bring him fresh food, such as pizza, ham, bread and fruit. After I had finished packing, my suitcase was loaded with 18 kilograms of food and books, with just a small bag for my own clothes.

When the day of my flight finally arrived, I just wanted to get on the plane and get it over with; I'm dreadful when it comes to saying farewells and even worse at air travel. After a tearful goodbye to Richard and my sons, I headed straight for the bar in the airport departure lounge, feeling thankful for the fact that it was about three o'clock in the afternoon. This meant I wouldn't look too odd ordering a double Cointreau on ice, which I desperately needed to settle my nerves. The stiff drink did the trick, and after a few minutes a kind of calmness settled over me. Before I knew it, I was sitting on the plane heading to Bangkok. I tried to rest during the flight but didn't get much sleep as my mind was busy with the thought of what awaited me. I really had no idea.

On touching down in Bangkok, I became very worried at what the Thai customs would make of the treasure trove of goodies in my overloaded suitcase. An 'overweight' sticker emblazoned my luggage, which might as well have been a red rag to the customs official, a shabby, middle-aged man in a well-worn shiny suit that had seen better days. After a few frantic minutes trying to explain the contents of my case, the customs officer finally became sick and tired of me explaining that I had a sick brother in prison who needed food, and must have thought to himself, 'Another stupid *farang*,' the Thai for 'foreigner', as I walked away.

Looking back, on that first trip I was so green about everything—about Thailand, about the prison system, about the ways of bureaucracy and the craziness of red tape. But that was to change and over the years I would become savvy, learning both the lingo and the lay of the land, including referring to the prison as 'the cook' or 'monkey house'. I also grew to understand the automatic assumption that anyone in the Thai prison system is there on drug charges, for as it turns out, 80% of prisoners are jailed for that reason. John was definitely an exception to the rule.

Walking out of the airport, the first thing to hit me in the face was the pollution; I'd never experienced anything like it. You could almost cut the air with a knife. I had heard that Bangkok had its environmental problems but nothing could have prepared me for the experience of walking into a clammy, choking city like this. I wasn't too put off because everybody seemed to be really friendly and polite, and I was thrilled at how lovely the Sofitel Hotel was. It was a relief to finally be at my destination, and I found myself thanking God for getting me to this point safe and sound.

Once in my room, I looked out my hotel window onto the city night-sky, trying to come to terms with where I was and why. Before my eyes, the glittering city dazzled me with its magnificence and beauty, and as I looked around at all the luxury and wealth of my hotel surroundings, I felt a twinge of regret that I had not come here for a more pleasant reason. John was suddenly so close, only eight kilometres down the road, but he was still a world away. All I wanted to do was sleep to make the next day come sooner, so I went straight to bed and prayed for oblivion until the morning. But instead I tossed and turned all night, still trying to comprehend that in a few hours I would be seeing my brother face to face.

At six o'clock the following morning, I got up, showered and turned on the television, looking out over the chaos of the locals inching their way along the freeway for another working day. I was overwhelmed by the endless skyline and the traffic jams that just went on forever. As I waited for time to pass, I kept compulsively checking my bag to make sure I had my passport, airline tickets and driver's license, all of which I would need at the prison. I also sorted out the food and gifts I had brought with me, trying to balance out the various items so John would have a variety to choose from on his first day. I was so nervous and excited that I couldn't contemplate the idea of eating breakfast and instead counted down the minutes until eight o'clock, when Embassy staff were due to meet me in the hotel foyer.

I was waiting in the foyer from eight sharp. Time ticked by painfully slowly and there was still no sign of anyone 15 minutes later. Waiting was agony. Then I noticed a young Thai man dart through the hotel doors. 'Debbie Singh?' he asked. When I confirmed that I was, he introduced himself as Kraisorn, an Embassy officer, and apologised for his lateness, citing the dreadful Bangkok traffic as the reason. He took me outside to where a mini van was waiting, with the Consul, Roy Clogston and another Embassy senior diplomat, Greg Rimes, inside. The Embassy staff were also taking the opportunity of the Klong Prem contact visits to visit Australian nationals, and while it was unusual for them to have a prisoner's family member accompany them, it had worked out this way in my case.

Getting into the minibus, finally on my way to the prison, triggered something that I'd been holding back. I tried so hard to be calm but my emotions got the better of me and I was suddenly too choked up to speak. Roy and Kraisorn gently attempted to prepare me for what I was about to experience, warning me that nothing they could say would be able to prepare me for the conditions of the prison, and that the best thing to do was to take what I saw in my stride, and not let it get to me. The enormity of the situation finally registered: I was on my way to the notorious Bangkok Hilton to see my brother, and I was terrified at what might await me when I got there.

We reached Klong Prem, where the staff told me to leave my bag in the van, as it wasn't permitted to bring it into the prison. I unthinkingly obeyed, forgetting that my passport was still in that very bag. I suddenly remembered this as the driver started to pull away. When I mentioned this, poor Kraisorn dashed after the driver and luckily succeeded in retrieving the bag. I wasn't aware then of what a risk I had exposed myself to and it was to be my first Thai lesson: *never* let your passport out of your sight. Every time you went to the prison, you had to present your passport, no matter how many times you'd been there already. Airline tickets were also regularly required. These were to prove the limited amount of time available to me as I pleaded for more time with my brother, but would also prove that everything was above board and that I was just a visitor in the country, and wasn't plotting anything underhanded.

My first impression of Klong Prem prison was that I had suddenly been transported to the set of a World War II movie where they were shooting the prisoner-of-war scenes. As we approached, I could see one of the watchtowers in the distance. It felt like my heart was going to jump out of my mouth; no amount of preparation steeled me against seeing the prison for the first time. It was frightening in its austerity, and seemed slightly surreal with its palm tree surrounds, orchids and pagoda-style huts in the wide open space before the main gates, as if it was simply dumped onto an area of natural beauty. The prison was built in 1940 and the outer facade is forbidding, a bleak wall of rundown stone and concrete with mould running up the walls and into the overwhelming darkness of the inner buildings. Dozens of mangy, stray dogs lazily sprawled around the front gates and through the gardens, sunning themselves. At the time, I wondered at their presence and how they were allowed to remain there, but I later learned that the King of Thailand is a dog-lover, thus for the Thai people, treating stray dogs well was a gesture of respect to their king. It was accepted by prison guards and the hundreds of mainly Thai visitors that this was the dogs' home and they had a right to be there, and thus they were left in peace. Flying proudly outside the prison was the Thai flag. It was an obvious but forceful reminder to me that this was a Thai institution on Thai soil, subject to Thai law—I almost felt as though the flag was a kind of message directed at me, saying that regardless of who you are and where you are from, this was Thailand, and Western ideals or hegemony didn't hold in this place. It was a lesson I learnt quick smart, and it's a reasonable one too.

Being tall and fair, I couldn't help but notice that I attracted a lot of attention from the Thai men, women and children. Most of it was very warm and there was an occasional fit of giggles from younger kids—after all, some people had travelled from the regional areas of Thailand where Westerners were still a rare sight. I soon learned that smiling and being gracious was the key to moving one step further in this culture. Manners are so important, and any kind of pushiness or impolite behaviour means that you are quickly stonewalled.

Once inside the prison walls, the heaviness of the air lent itself to an overwhelming sense of oppression, anguish and defeat. Coils of barbed wire sat atop the six metre high walls and guard towers overlooked every action on the ground. Khaki-clad prison officers in aviator-style sunglasses seemed to be everywhere, casually swinging truncheons as they strolled through the grounds. The whole place just seemed awful.

I took a deep breath and walked towards the sign-in area. I waited as Kraisorn sorted out the paperwork. The guard, Somphon, whom I would come to know well over the coming years, was inscrutable, seemingly emotionless and giving nothing away, although I somehow had a feeling that behind the mask, he did feel for my situation. Then it was time to hand over the bag of food for inspection. Guards at tables inspected all goods being brought into the prison, and I watched them go through the various items I had bought for John. The clothing and books were not allowed to come into the prison, for reasons I still don't know to this day, but I was told that I could take these things away and then post them to the prison via the Embassy. Thankfully, most of the food was passed, apart from the glass jars and tins, which were rejected as the containers could be fashioned into weapons. That was another hard lesson learnt, but as long as the staple Australian treats, the Cherry Ripes and Twisties made it through, I knew John would be happy with his haul.

We passed through three sets of gates into amazing, manicured gardens with topiary and lots of bougainvillea splashing colour everywhere. A prisoner once described these gardens as 'putting nice face on things' and the contrast between this luxuriance and the prison interior was striking. The swathe of tropical plants and ponds brimming with Koi fish are the part of the prison designed for the public eye; the cramped and stinking concrete cages are a very different vista. I was in a daze as we walked through the prison gardens, my ears assaulted by the sound of a prison officer screeching in Thai through a loud speaker—the volume was deafening and I wondered what in the world he could be saying that was so important. The scene was so strange and foreign. In the distance to the left I could see a group of Westerners huddled under a tarpaulin bivouac, together in their loneliness, and on the right were hundreds of Thai inmates and family members hugging and openly weeping, the younger ones kowtowing to their elders. As these visits were only allowed once a year this was understandably an extremely important occasion for both the inmates and those coming to see loved ones. I guessed the Westerners had nobody coming to see them and were forced to sit there and watch the other inmates meet their families and loved ones for a few bittersweet hours. I felt a twinge of pity and sadness for them. *How long had it been since they saw someone they loved?*

Looking around, I could see this place was dreadful and oppressive, and knew that my own impressions wouldn't even begin to describe what lay behind this supposedly welcoming facade put on for visitors. I shuddered to think of what lay beneath. Like the Thai people around me, I found myself shaking with emotion. Trying to settle the thousands of butterflies doing somersaults in the pit of my stomach, I rapidly scanned the many people congregating around me before my eyes rested on a tall, gangly, bespectacled figure in the distance who could only be my brother. His reed-thin frame was fifty metres away and I left the Embassy representatives to rush to him, walking as fast as I could, stepping over the open sewer and onto a piece of cardboard which almost, but not quite, saved me from being ankle deep in mud. It was the wet season and cardboard paths had been strewn across the visiting area, as the ground itself was so spongy. Most of the people were up to their ankles in thick dark mud. Again, my inexperience and first-timer status was evident; I was wearing sandals that were totally inappropriate for the conditions at that time of year.

Finally, John and I were face to face and I got the shock of my life. I fell into his arms and sobbed like a child. He had never carried a lot of weight, but I saw instantly that over the last two years he had wasted away into a shadow of himself. As I clutched him to me, all I could feel was bones. I could feel his spine sticking through the thin material of his shirt. As I pulled myself away and looked up to his face, I noticed that his broken glasses were lopsided, held together by a piece of wire. Then he smiled at me, and to my horror I saw that his top teeth had rotted away. Half of them were missing and what were left were black stumps. My heart broke and I wept uncontrollably, wracked with anguish at what had been done to our John. Here he was, looking like something out of a concentration camp, all for a stupid act and a thousand bucks.

Common sense prevailed and I knew I had to pull myself together. Becoming over-emotional wasn't going to help matters. I forced myself to recover from the initial shock of John's physical deterioration, and we sat down to talk. Before we really got into it, John asked if I would like a soft drink and walked off to the refreshments area. Almost immediately, a very tall, thin guy in his mid-forties with a long ginger beard appeared in front of me. Strangely, I remember him as bearing a striking resemblance to the TV character, Cat Weasel. He sat down in John's seat as though it was his right to do so. In an Australian accent, he introduced himself to me, told me that he knew our John, and that my brother had told him how much he was looking forward to my visit. As we chatted, we talked about the various ways of getting out of Klong Prem, one of which was obtaining a Royal Pardon from the King of Thailand. When our conversation shifted to the Australian Embassy, he began a verbal assault against the Embassy staff, telling me how much he hated them. He claimed that they had conspired against him to keep him imprisoned and had all but thrown away the key. That wasn't what I wanted to hear. It was clear this guy was pretty unbalanced.

Then John returned, his hands clasped around three cups of Coke. He had got me two cups in case I needed another, saying he did not want to waste any more of our precious visiting time queuing for drinks. The other inmate got up and left us to it, and John sat back down. Over the years that followed, I realised that amongst the prisoners, the nature of the individual charges were immaterial and no one really cared who was in for what reason, as more often than not it was a drug charge anyway. But at the time, it was all new to me and I asked John if he knew the type of offence for which the inmate had been convicted. I certainly was not prepared for the answer he gave me. The man was a paedophile who, after serving time in Australia had fled to Thailand to continue his vice, and now had a string of convictions in both countries. In my naïveté, I was shocked and disgusted that I had given such a person the time of day and felt strangely tainted by association. John went on to outline some of the truly horrific crimes this man had committed. It seemed fundamentally wrong that inside the prison this guy was treated no better or worse than someone like John, who was in for a petty crime.

There seemed no concept of scale in the Thai justice system, no shades of grey, no punishment to fit the crime, with all lawbreakers, whether their crime was heinous or relatively inconsequential, all together on an equal footing. This unsettling fact made me worry even more. What kind of people did he have to share a cell with?

John had told me that he shared a cell with 30 other men in stifling conditions, and slept on the floor using clothes as a pillow. This was bad enough, but to think what some of these other men were in for, and sharing a cell with my little brother, was just an awful thought.

Over the next precious hour, John and I talked about many things, but mainly about John's health and getting him some new glasses. I remember that we even managed a few laughs, talking just like any brother and sister, as John told me about some of the cultural contradictions and differences in Thailand. It turned out that the man shouting through the loudspeaker had been instructing everyone to enjoy themselves! We also laughed at the prison band playing in the visiting area which, though a nice touch, sure made conversation a lot more difficult. It was during this visit that I made a promise to my brother that I would do whatever I could to get him out of Klong Prem. I said I would never walk away and leave him there, and that I would fight for his release, whatever the cost. What a promise it turned out to be! One that was to irrevocably change my life and set me on a surreal and often stormy journey in the years that followed. But I was glad I made it. I was leaving John with the message that he was not alone, and that I wouldn't forget about him. More importantly, I was giving him hope that some day I might find a way to get him out of here and bring him back to Australia.

All too soon our allotted hour was up and it was time for me to leave. We both tried to put on a brave face and I said goodbye until the next day. I walked away sobbing, no longer caring about the strange looks I was getting from the Thai guards, as I seemed to be the only foreign visitor apart from the Embassy staff. At the time, it struck me as merely odd, but as I became more familiar with the Thai prison system, I realised how many foreign nationals were left for dead in this prison system, and how sad it was that they existed in such terrible conditions with little outside support.

Once outside the prison, I caught up with the Embassy representatives who were waiting for me. The words tumbled out of my mouth as I stressed the urgency behind getting medical attention for John. I blurted out what John had told me during the visit; that he believed he had contracted tuberculosis and had asked that a request be put in for him to be visited by the Australian doctor attached to the Embassy as soon as possible. Roy assured me that this would happen.

Arriving back at the hotel, I was absolutely exhausted. This first visit to John had left me feeling physically and emotionally drained. I felt as though I had a thick fog in my head and it was all I could do to lie down on the bed; I couldn't even summon the energy to take a much-needed shower. The prison clothing requirements of trousers and covered shoulders in such oppressive heat meant that I was hot, sweaty and uncomfortable, but I desperately wanted to sleep and then wake up with a clear head, as it seemed so important that I start thinking straight. My eyelids dropped and I must have slept for two hours.

When I opened my eyes, my waking thoughts were that I had to get myself into action and try to order some spectacles for John. With a bit of luck, I thought, I might even be able to bring them to the prison the next day. I wandered over to the shopping complex next to my hotel and soon found an optometrist, where to my delight the shop attendant told me that in two hours and for approximately AU$150 John's glasses would be ready.

I roamed around the shopping centre feeling much more positive. The boost of knowing that I could make a practical difference to John's quality of life, even on a small scale, was just what I needed. But still playing on my mind was the shocking state of John's teeth. I could not leave Bangkok without making some inquiries about the possibility of him having some dental work done from inside or outside the prison. Unexpectedly, as though fate was playing into my hands, I came across a dental surgery. I stood outside and the flashback of seeing John in such a state flooded my mind, as clearly as if he was standing in front of me. Tears welled in my eyes and before I knew it I was inside the surgery asking for some information. A young Thai girl who did not speak English greeted me, and quickly disappeared to find a staff member who could help me. I was clearly distressed and when the woman asked me if she could help me, my words stuck in my throat. Before I knew it I succumbed to another wracking flood of tears. Sobbing and in broken sentences, I tried to explain John's situation. The shop attendant was very sympathetic, although of course there was absolutely nothing she could do except tell me I needed to speak to the prison about John's teeth. I knew she was right, and that she couldn't help. It was crazy of me to go in there in the first place, but I was desperate to talk to someone, anyone with a tenuous connection to the problem. I knew that I was being irrational and not making any sense, grabbing at straws. Feeling embarrassed and stupid, I thanked her and left the surgery with my head bowed, quietly weeping. All I wanted was to get back to my hotel room and hide from the world.

My emotions were swinging between extreme highs and lows like one of those amusement park rides. Little victories would buoy me and seem so significant, but a setback would plunge me into despair. Feeling helpless to do anything about John's teeth upset me no end. I sat down on the bed and my mind kept comparing John's living conditions just eight kilometres down the road, to my situation, as I sat with every creature comfort available to me in my luxurious hotel room. It was impossible to deal with. Looking back, I think this day was a significant turning point in many ways. My self-indulgence became glaringly clear—I was bemoaning my inability to help John, yet this wasn't doing anyone any good at all! It was time to stop feeling sorry for myself and to focus all my energies on changing the situation. I could hide away and cry myself to sleep, or I could get my emotions in order and start turning this negative state of affairs into a positive one. I wasn't helpless, I wasn't useless, and there were so many things I might be able to do. So with a deep breath, and masking my tear stained face with my sunglasses, I set out from the hotel once again, this time to collect John's spectacles. Holding them in my hand, I focused on imagining him wearing them when I took them to him the next day. It felt important to be able to help in some small way, to see that something was going right.

Roy and Kraisorn had told me to keep in touch, so later that day I called the Embassy to make an appointment to talk about John and to find out what was needed for an application for a Royal Pardon, which according to my preliminary research seemed to be John's only hope of getting out of Klong Prem. When I met with Roy, I discovered that once the documentation was ready to submit, the Pardon application could take up to two years to reach the King's office. My heart sank at this setback in my plans, but what choice did we have? Two years was better than the eight John still had to serve, so over the next few days I met again with Roy at the Embassy. I wanted as much information as possible about the Pardon application, and Roy showed me a copy of another Australian applicant, to give me an idea of what was needed. This was very helpful and I left brimming with ideas and a list of documents to follow up.

At night in my hotel room, I prepared lists of the people I needed to contact when I got back home; members of parliament, doctors, family members. I felt heartened by the fact that we could do something positive for John, although he himself had told me that he had absolutely no faith in ever being granted a Pardon, that there was nothing anybody could do. His pessimism on this front meant that he showed little interest in helping prepare the application, so I decided to do it for him. That's what big sisters are for. I also contacted the British Embassy, as John still held dual citizenship and had been visited by British Embassy staff. I found out that the UK had a Prisoner Exchange Treaty in place, so I called the Embassy and made contact with a very helpful lady called Kate Duffel, who coincidentally happened to be an Australian. She faxed me a copy of the British-Thai Treaty and was very sympathetic. But if we went down the British path and were successful, John would be transferred to a UK prison, so I wasn't sure that this was the best path to take.

The Australian Embassy had sought permission through the Thai Corrections Department for me to have two contact visits with John and non-contact visits on the other days. On the request paperwork the words 'Embassy room' were highlighted. The Embassy room was a small wooden building, clean and air-conditioned, where staff from many embassies would meet their incarcerated nationals. But things proved to be hit and miss. I would turn up at the prison every day with the hope that Mr Somphon would allow me a visit. I learnt very quickly that the rules changed on a daily basis, and not to take anything for granted, for disappointment was inevitable. I joined the long queue each day, trembling with nerves and on the verge of tears. Although this tenuous state of affairs was normal practice, it seemed so heartless, waiting with your hopes up, often for more than an hour, to know your fate for the day.

One day as I waited, I got talking to an Iranian woman whose husband was in Klong Prem after being caught with hash. She travelled from Singapore every month to see her husband, and assisted me on a few occasions by providing valuable information about which queue to join, pointing out the friendly guards, and who was best to avoid. It paid to always have your airline ticket with you at these times, as it proved to the guard that you were genuinely here in Bangkok to visit your loved one or friend, and on more than one occasion it got me an extra non-contact visit. I was lucky; for most days Mr Somphon gave me a pass to have non-contact visits, and even though they were only 20 minutes long, I made the most of every second I had with my brother.

It didn't take long to realise that most Thais, regardless of class, show respect and expect it back. I was very comfortable with this, having been brought up with the same values. I saw first hand that many foreigners treated Thais with utter contempt and disrespect, especially some men towards Thai women, and this revolted me. I couldn't understand it. Even in the prison, I witnessed several foreign visitors, on the rare occasions there were some, treating the prison officers with rudeness, arrogance and disrespect. It wasn't in my nature to act that way, and I also knew you could catch more bees with honey than with vinegar, so on returning to Australia I sent Mr Somphon a card, thanking him for his kindness.

While at the prison, I figured out that a smile and a *wai*, bowing your head with your hands in a prayer position, opened doors for me on my first visit and every one after that. I also quickly learned that addressing people with their appropriate titles showed respect too. All of this I found hard to remember, but I took it all down in a daily diary, to memorise whenever I could find the time.

* * *

The stress and tension of seeing John for the first time in quite a while, and of seeing him in such a state, had taken a massive toll on me emotionally, and I felt drained. I felt I needed to get away from the horrible mental images that had become stored in my mind on my trip to Klong Prem, and decided to get into the city to take in its atmosphere. I had to admit, I was intrigued by Bangkok; by its sights and sounds. It's not the cleanest or safest place in the world, but I warmed to it straight away and tried from the start to embrace the people and the culture. It was a gamble that I think paid off. I was constantly surprised as I walked the streets, trying to clear my head, seeing something strange and sometimes startling on every street corner. I knew it would take a while to get used to this place; it all seemed so alien to me. There was an edge to the atmosphere here, more than any place I had been before, where excitement and energy mixed with a sort of seedy nervousness, where everything had a price because money talked, and sex was for sale everywhere you looked. Everything seemed out in the open, yet nothing was what it seemed. Bars could be brothels on closer inspection, run-down shacks stood next to shopping malls, and a single wrong turn could lead you down a darkened alley to a seedy underworld. Yet to me, Bangkok was alive with energy and I was taken in by it completely.

At about five o'clock in the afternoon, the mood in Silom Road changed dramatically. Thai people emerged from nowhere, setting up their stalls at Patpong Market and lugging around huge metal boxes filled with counterfeit handbags, clothing and anything else they could sell to the thousands of tourists who would soon start to flood through the narrow paths and lane ways. Traditional Thai food stalls were being set up everywhere, but my biggest surprise came when what had looked like closed and empty shop fronts suddenly had flashing colour lights illuminating them like Christmas trees, and disco music booming from inside. The penny suddenly dropped and it dawned on me why the receptionist at my very respectable hotel had looked at me very oddly when he realised I was planning a visit to Patpong and asked how to get there—my query would have been the equivalent of asking directions to a King's Cross brothel, multiplied tenfold! It was Bangkok's most notorious GoGo bar district, and although there was indeed a market, I soon realised the real business wasn't in counterfeit handbags, and that especially here, pretty much anything was on sale, for a price.

Again, my appearance made me stand out as a bit of a novelty with the street traders, and on this and later trips I was astonished at how they, the taxi men and all of the locals took to me when I told them I was from Liverpool. It won me many friends and I was proud to realise just how big Liverpool FC are in Thailand. One mention of Liverpool and their eyes would light up. 'Ah, Michael Owen, Liverpool number one,' they'd enthusiastically offer as I smiled back at them. The Beatles got a lot of mentions too, and I was happy to go along with it if it made me fit in better.

As darkness set in, it occurred to me that I had better make my way back to the hotel on the outskirts of the city. If I hadn't been by myself I probably would have stayed longer to take in this mad scene, but getting home to my family in one piece was a priority. After all, just venturing on this journey to Thailand was a giant step for me. *Don't push your luck*, I thought. In the back of a taxi, where I was to spend a lot of my time over the next few years, I furiously wrote down everything I had learned, noticed or picked up so far, before it left my overloaded brain forever. I continued to do this on later trips, so that I could fit in as much as I could and to make sure I showed everybody the respect they deserved. This proved to be my very own survival kit.

Arriving safely back at the hotel, I settled in for the evening, my head filled with the amazing and exotic sights I had seen that day. I was happy I had managed to see another side of Bangkok apart from the prison walls and the hotel, and I imagined John's surprise when I would tell him of my adventure the next day before flying home.

My final contact visit with John proved to be the hardest part of my first trip to Bangkok. Although we laughed and chattered about good and bad things, and I got to see his face light up as I handed him a brand new pair of glasses, the point where we had to say goodbye was nothing short of nightmarish. How could I possibly walk away and leave him there? When would I ever see him again? And what state would he be in? I was trying very hard to keep myself together for his sake, but in many ways coming to Bangkok had made the situation much worse for me, now that I knew where I was leaving John, seeing the awful conditions, and knowing what he would suffer until I could get him out. Just the idea of walking away from him was devastating. But still, there was an upside, and I needed to focus on that to tide me over. We had achieved so much in one week: John had got his food, new glasses that would improve his quality of life in the prison so much, and a visit from a family member, when there were inmates who had not received a visit for years, and who were serving such ridiculously long sentences that it wasn't even certain that they would come out alive. This thought stayed with me long after I left John behind.

I cried all the way back to the hotel. My poor taxi driver was so kind to me; he kept asking me if I was okay, and seemed genuinely concerned. Little gestures of humanity like this helped so much, and the power of the kindness of strangers should never be underestimated. I had one hour to sort myself out before leaving for the airport. Although right now I needed to get home to my husband and my boys, and again assume my role of wife, mother and businesswoman, these roles would now be coloured with the awareness that life would never be the same again.

— CHAPTER THREE —

Although leaving John behind in Bangkok was one of the hardest things I ever had to do in my life, I did my best to console myself in the taxi on the way to the airport, telling myself that I would somehow make it back to Thailand before too long. At the same time, my emotions were still wildly seesawing—as much as I didn't want to leave John in his desperate situation, a little more than a week spent away from my family had seemed like forever and I could barely wait for the moment when the plane touched down on Perth soil so I could be with the boys and my husband. It was a guilty kind of excitement.

But after returning home from my emotional rollercoaster, I found it hard to sleep, eat and get back into the normality of the family life I had left behind just eight days earlier. It felt like I had come back from another world. My family was keen to know how John was faring, and opening up to them was hard to do in the first few days. How could I describe how dreadful the prison was? Or how bad John looked? Looking back, I think the surreal situation I had just experienced took a little while to process and I was shell-shocked. The trauma of witnessing John in such a dire state of health and seeing first hand the dreadful conditions in which he was living had impacted on me more than I had realised. Telling the rest of the family about it made the nightmare seem more real, and I found it hard that I had to continually relive my experience each time.

At first, I couldn't bear to tell my parents the truth. I didn't want to lie, but telling them the horrible details of John's health and conditions was only going to cause them pain. I tried to play it down, saying he was very thin and that when I met him first his glasses were hanging on with a piece of wire, and that his teeth looked very bad, but I never mentioned the T.B. My parents weren't too keen on me going to Bangkok alone in the first place, so to justify the trip I sang out all the positive stuff before they had time to digest what I had told them. I mentioned how I had been able to get John a new pair of glasses within a day, that I'd made enquiries about him seeing a dentist in the prison, and that I was able to load him up with food and put money in his bank account.

This seemed to do the trick and we were soon talking about having a family whip-round to pay for John's dental work. I was relieved to get out some of what I had seen, but the guilt at not telling them the scale of the situation was churning up my insides. I still needed to tell them the truth about the length of John's sentence, but straight after this first trip was not the time.

Thinking about my brother's situation filled my waking hours and regularly penetrated my dreams. From the outset, I constantly questioned what I was doing—*was I putting John before my husband and kids? What was happening to my priorities and the commitments I had already made to others in my life, whom I loved dearly?* And despite all that was happening, I was back at work and quickly falling into my old routine, physically doing all the things I used to do, though my headspace was divided between Bangkok and Perth. Although I had returned home with a to-do list regarding John's Pardon application, I felt it was so important to get back on track with my family and my business, addressing the neglect they had suffered over the past months when I had invested all my time into preparing for the trip to Bangkok. On top of everything, Richard was still working away in the mines, working two weeks on, one week off, so I simply had to hold my end when he was away. Juggling the various roles kept me sane, in that it prevented me from dwelling too deeply on John's circumstances, though he was never far from my mind.

Still, I had returned from Bangkok with a head full of ideas of how I could help John get out of that hell, and while I made sure I was still carrying my weight at work and home, I kept up my campaign of phone calls to DFAT and the Australian Embassy. My new focus, after learning of the British/Thai Transfer Treaty, was to ascertain the status of an Australian prisoner exchange treaty with Thailand. All I could find out was that it had been tabled in parliament in 1997, and that some prisoners' relatives had made submissions on why the Bill should be passed. Two years had passed and from what I could work out, it seemed that no further progress had been made and the whole process had ground to a halt. I was making phone calls to Perth lawyers, Amnesty International and anyone else who I thought might help, or at the very least would listen to what I had to say. But it was a hard slog trying to convince people that this was urgent and important, and my enquiries weren't getting me anywhere. It constantly felt as though doors were being slammed in my face. After banging my head against too many walls, I decided it was time to take matters into my own hands. Obviously the Transfer Treaty wasn't on anyone's radar and I needed to start from scratch. I'm a pretty determined person, and if I aim to do something, I do it. And I was determined to keep working on helping John. I felt responsible for him. He was my little brother. Many different family members had had enough of him in the past and said he was a taker, not a giver, but I didn't care. I wanted him back, safe. One day in the shop, I sat quietly, and methodically put together a list of the MPs and government departments I should contact on John's behalf. It was time to get down to some serious business.

Over the months following my visit, John's letters were a lot more positive. I knew the family contact had made a huge difference to his mental state, and Mum and I kept up the parcels and letters, as well as sending money via DFAT in Canberra while I plodded along, gathering whatever information I could. Almost anything to do with Thai prisons or the mere mention of the word 'Bangkok' would stop me in my tracks. My ever-growing list of contacts at various government departments meant that I was fast running out of pages in my address book, so I decided it was time for me to join the twenty-first century and buy a computer. I had never touched a keyboard in my life, e-mail was a complete mystery, and a crash course in all things technological was desperately required. But what a revelation! My computer screen soon became my window to the world, and I would stay up until the early hours of every morning e-mailing everyone I thought might be able to help me and, more importantly, scouring the internet, hunting for information on Thai prisons, tuberculosis treatments, Australian law and Thai customs in general. I wanted to find out how the country worked in every way, and read everything I could about all aspects of Thai culture, especially if it had anything to do with foreigners in Thailand. In fact, anything related to John's situation was fair game and knowing that knowledge was power, I researched relentlessly and amassed an arsenal of information.

I also drafted a sample Royal Pardon application letter to the King of Thailand, based on the information I had gathered, and began making appointments with various people, including my local Liberal MP. This particular meeting started on a pretty low note, as when greeting me for the first time, he addressed me as 'Mrs Curry'. Given that my married name is Singh, a common Indian name, it appeared that he'd used a memory aid and had blundered spectacularly. In any case, I was pretty sure I was on to a loser. He drafted a letter that at first glance looked impressive. It was a great feeling to see the official letterhead and the weight of some parliamentary support backing John's case. Then I read it.

The protocol of his letter was correct; he had addressed his plea to the King of Thailand and so on, but then he started to waffle on about his visit earlier that year to the Thamkrabok Monastery outside Bangkok. Thamkrabok was an alternative drug rehabilitation program. I was gutted to think this apparently educated man could relate John's crime of traveller's cheque fraud to drug possession and smuggling cases in Thailand, and more significantly, to do so in the letter that was designed to help him. John's case, if anything, required distancing from any taint of drugs because his offence was special in that it *wasn't* a drug case. This letter was only going to make it worse. Needless to say, I was crushed, and that correspondence never made it to the King—instead it ended up in the bin. My confidence in political support was wavering. I couldn't seem to find anyone who really understood, or, more to the point, who really cared. It was more than obvious by this stage that opinions on Thai prisons wasn't a platform that was going to bring in more votes, and so it was way down the list of priorities for most politicians.

Feeling frustrated at my experience with my Liberal MP, I decided to try another political avenue, a senator who had an office in the same complex as my shop. Senator Jim McKiernan seemed to be more knowledgeable about how I should approach matters dealing with the federal government, and he proved to be a valuable ally later, bringing John's case to the attention of parliament at a crucial moment. But wading through the bureaucracy was such a slow process and I was becoming increasingly impatient. I was still gathering letters of support from family members and friends and I was constantly writing to John. Just receiving a letter from him gave me the incentive to carry on, as I hoped his receiving one from me was doing the same.

One of my best internet finds in these early days was an article about a doctor who had worked at John's prison in Bangkok for the past twenty years. His name was Dr John Lerwitworapong. I jotted down his contact details and the next day I nervously tapped out his phone number. My words spilled into themselves as I introduced myself and explained why I was calling. He was on the receiving end of a confused barrage before I finally let him get a word in edgeways. Hearing the tremor in my voice and recognising my anxiety, Dr John went to great pains to calm me and promised that he would summon John to the hospital and x-ray him. I always recall the unreal nature of that conversation—it seemed unbelievable that I was sitting in my home in Australia talking with the Klong Prem prison doctor about my brother's case of TB, and the doctor turned out to be so compassionate and the best kind of humanitarian. I was so happy and felt for the first time in ages I was finally getting somewhere. Direct contact had got me somewhere that no amount of phone calls to the Embassy had achieved.

A few days later when I returned home from work, I put down my bags of grocery shopping and in what had fast become routine, I raced to the computer to check if I had any e-mails from Canberra or Thailand. As usual, dinner would just have to wait! Dr John's unpronounceable name blazed across my screen in my inbox, and on opening his e-mail, I was happily stunned to discover that he had taken two photographs of John in the hospital grounds and sent them to me. John's thin frame was in front of me, wearing a blue T-shirt, his arms folded, a kind of wry smile on his face. The immediacy of it was wonderful—it felt as though Dr John had thrown me a lifeline. John had started a six-month course of drugs to treat his tuberculosis and Dr John's e-mail reassured me that he would continue to call up John for monthly x-rays to monitor the scarring on his lungs caused by the disease. I could not wait to tell Mum and Dad. This development was so encouraging, as it hammered home that I could make a real difference, even though I was only one person, and so far away. The tyranny of distance seemed to slide into insignificance.

Dr John proved himself to be invaluable. This man was a true humanitarian who lived and breathed his prison hospital role, and after many years of fundraising, a new hospital in Klong Prem was officially opened in 2004. He takes such an honest and heartfelt interest in the lives of those he treats and doesn't discriminate against anyone— he just lives to heal and make people's lives better. Those little things like an e-mailed picture were so special—I never would have thought that they could happen. And I really believe that without Dr John's help, John would not have received any assistance.

Time continued to pass and in June 2000, I received a letter from DFAT advising me that the next opportunity for contact visits would be in August. This time there was no question in my heart. I simply had to go. With the letter still in my hand, I called Mum to let her know. Without hesitation she said she would like to come to Bangkok with me, and before the day was over, both of us were booked on a flight to Thailand.

I remember feeling terribly anxious about what John would say about Mum coming to Bangkok and seeing him in this horrendous situation, but decided to be straight up. I quickly fired off a letter telling him that both of us were coming to visit, hoping for the best. In the meantime, Mum was buying up big on Cherry Ripe bars, Vegemite and anything else she thought John might like.

I called DFAT and informed them that both Mum and I would be going to see John for the contact visits. I sensed that the Australian Embassy staff in Bangkok might not be so thrilled, as over the recent months I had had some pretty frosty phone calls with Roy, the Consul. I know the last thing the Embassy wanted was a prisoner's family breathing down their necks, constantly asking questions and demanding answers and action, but as they didn't seem to be capable of independently forcing the issue, I felt I was left with no other choice but to keep hassling them for progress.

It was not long after we had booked our flights that I was at home browsing through our local weekend paper, *The Sunday Times*. As is the case when something becomes a part of one's life, by this stage anything remotely connected to Thailand leapt out from the print and grabbed my attention. I was soon engrossed in a story about a Catholic nun from Perth by the name of Sister Joan Evans. Sister Joan had lived in the Bangkok slums for some time, helping the slum dwellers in their day-to-day struggle to survive. I was immediately struck by this wonderful woman's compassion and I rang Mum to let her know about the article. I wasn't telling her anything she didn't already know—she had already read the story with the same sense of excitement and we both agreed that we should at least try to get in touch with her.

Feeling brave, I contacted Sister Joan's Perth convent, asking if it was possible to get her contact details and enquiring how we might be able to help her cause. The nuns passed on a phone number and e-mail address, and that night I sent an e-mail, explaining our story and asking if Mum and I might have the opportunity of meeting her when we were next in Bangkok. Sister Joan soon replied and was very warm and generous, and over the next month or so we kept in touch through e-mail and phone calls. To say this first contact was the beginning of a special friendship is an understatement —this relationship is now a pivotal part of my life.

June moved into July and one day as I was working in my shop, I heard a radio news bulletin that an Australian prisoner from Klong Prem had been granted a Royal Pardon on the grounds of terminal illness. I raced off to buy our daily newspaper, hoping for an article with more details. Sure enough, the news story was in the daily edition and after reading it, I found myself on the phone to the *The West Australian* newspaper, begging for more information. Although they could not pass on any more information, they took my phone number with a promise that someone would get back to me. True to their word, within five minutes a reporter named Ruth Callaghan called me, asking if it was possible to meet, to talk about highlighting John's case.

I listened to her request with some trepidation, for up until this point only close family and friends knew about John's situation and for John's sake we had deliberately avoided going to the press. In addition, if I was to go ahead with this, it meant that I finally had to come clean with my parents and tell them the actual length of John's sentence. Up until this point, media involvement definitely wasn't the course the family thought we should take, so I explained to Ruth I would have to speak with my parents before I could agree to meet with her. Telling my parents the truth about John's sentence was something I knew I had to do. It would be a great relief to get that off my chest and move on, but I was not looking forward to it.

I didn't want to create any further dramas or heartbreak, so I told Mum on her own first. I tried to break it to her in a positive way, if there was one, saying that although John's sentence was actually ten years, not two, he had just had it reduced to eight years. I looked at her with a sideways glance as I waited for her to react. She looked shocked, but told me she knew I had been holding something back all this time. She was visibly shaken, but I was glad to see she just wanted to know what we could do to get him home. She seemed more worried about how Dad would react, and so was I.

I talked it over with her, and decided to bite the bullet and tell him. Again, I gave him the positive spiel and then blurted out the truth. John had ten years, not two, but it was now eight. It was lucky he was sitting down at the time, because I was sure he would have collapsed. He hit the roof, fuming at the Australian government for not helping John more in the early stages. This was the moment I had dreaded, but I felt like I had defused a time bomb in my head. It would take time, but I knew life would go on and the fight for John's freedom would now go up a notch.

Even with that hurdle overcome, I knew any mention of media interest would send Mum and Dad into a spin, so I approached them about this subject walking on eggshells. I was careful to outline all the positive aspects of using the media to bring attention to John's plight and put pressure on those with the power to change things, and as I expected, I was met with a barrage of potential negative outcomes. My parents were very wary of taking this path. Although they never explicitly agreed with this change in tack, Dad's final words were, 'We'll leave it up to you.'

With my parents' acceptance, if not their approval, I called Ruth and we arranged to meet the next day at my home. I was so nervous that I had two glasses of wine before she arrived, and when I realised that she had a photographer accompanying her, I broke out into a cold sweat. Thankfully Ruth was lovely, possessing a genuinely caring nature and I felt totally at ease talking to her. After we had finished, the photographer took a picture of me reading John's letters and with much relief when it was all over, I saw them out my front door, glad the interview was over and done with, but still nervous about how John's story would be represented. Though I was fairly confident that Ruth wouldn't sensationalise the article, I was a bundle of nerves as I waited for the newspaper the following day, praying that I had done the right thing.

My instinct proved correct and Ruth's article was fine —it outlined John's situation and highlighted the fact that a transfer treaty was the only thing that could change his situation. The photograph of me certainly caught the eye and during the next day at work, a steady stream of customers came into my shop, asking me if the story about our John was true. Most were very sympathetic, and this was reassuring. I also hoped that going public would stop the whispers and innuendo that John was involved in drugs and I was glad that the article clearly stated that his crime was traveller's cheque fraud. By this point, I had given up on anyone who refused to believe the real reason why he was in jail and cut them out of my life. I just didn't need their negativity. Mum and Dad also seemed reasonably happy with the write-up and I think they too were relieved that it was out in the open. Later that day, Ruth called to let me know that a lady named Julie Dabala had phoned *The West Australian* and asked Ruth to pass on her phone number. She explained that Julie visited the prisons in Bangkok and had Australian friends over there who might be of some help to us. I was very grateful because I felt I needed all the help I could get. Julie and her friends visited inmates in the Thai prisons and really revealed to me the importance of prisoners having somebody visit them. They provided food and money for those most in need, but most importantly they provided a person to talk to for the many people who didn't even have that from one end of the year to the other. I thought back to my visit to John, when I had seen the foreign prisoners sitting under a tarpaulin, looking so lonely, and wondered when was the last time they had seen a friendly face. The thought had never really left my head, and seeing how much improvement there was in John's attitude when he received even a letter from me just underlined the importance for the foreign prisoners of having someone to talk to. It seemed that Julie knew this too.

Mum and I travelled to Bangkok as planned in August, but this time there was another dimension to our trip. Although seeing John and taking care of his needs was undoubtedly our first priority, knowing we were going to meet Sister Joan was a special and invigorating bonus and we were keen to learn more about Bangkok beyond its prison system. After a good flight that enabled us to spend some really solid time together after many years, Mum and I arrived in the evening and went straight to the Sofitel. The hotel was already starting to feel like a home away from home; nothing seemed to have changed since my visit the previous year, and I was greeted by familiar staff with the same smiling faces. On our arrival, I called Sister Joan to let her know we had arrived safely and was greeted with an upbeat response as she told me how much she was looking forward to meeting both of us.

We unpacked our bags and then tumbled exhausted into our beds, far too tired to worry about the next day.

When we got up the next morning, our first stop was the local supermarket. Learning from my first prison visit, I had worked out that I could still get things like Vegemite, peanut butter and other tinned goods in to John, if we scooped the food into plastic containers to make it 'legal'. As we worked together, emptying the contents of the suitcases bursting with food and books for John and packing them carefully into plastic bags, I also spent the morning mentally preparing. Although I had been through this on my earlier trip, it was so different doing this with Mum. I had very mixed emotions, and was constantly worrying about what was going through Mum's head. How would she cope with seeing John for the first time in five years, and in these awful circumstances? How could I prepare her for what lay ahead?

Just before midday, we left for the prison, weighed down with John's treasure trove of food. We attracted some bemused looks from the staff at our posh hotel, who must have wondered what these women were up to, going to the local 'monkey house'. We arrived at the prison at noon on Monday, 7 August 2000, ahead of our one o'clock visit, to give us time to complete the complex paperwork.

As the taxi pulled past the gates and into Klong Prem, I turned to Mum and asked her if she was okay. She gave me a nod, but remained silent. I don't think she could get the words out. Thankfully, all the red tape side of things went smoothly and I was relieved to see the familiar face of Mr Somphon, the officer who had been so kind to me the previous year, giving me extra non-contact passes when he knew how distressed I had been by finding my brother in such bad health, and that I had travelled alone from Australia.

Inside the prison entrance, we joined the long queue of people waiting to deposit the food brought for the prisoners. We were then directed to another queue to go through the next set of gates to the visiting area. I surreptitiously stole a glance at Mum, who seemed to be coping well. This time the visiting area was outside, with plastic tables and chairs set up on a grassy space, in a vast improvement on last year's effort. We sat down and Mum lit a cigarette. I took in the surroundings and it was a strange scene indeed, like a surreal garden fete. A guard caught my attention, pointing to a tall, blonde, healthy-looking guy who was approaching us, but even from a distance it was obvious it wasn't John and we told the guard so. Nevertheless, the guy continued to walk towards us, came forward and introduced himself. He told us his name was Evan, he was from Estonia and that John would be coming soon. As if on cue, John appeared from nowhere, and Mum leapt up and embraced him. I could see she was shocked by his appearance; she struggled to take in the horrible fact that this bag of bones standing in front of her, with rotten teeth as he tried to smile at her, was her son, but she tried her best to appear strong for him. He just stood there, a dangerously frail and weakened man, like a little boy in front of his mother, needing her comfort and support. What made it an even more emotional meeting between Mum and John than even these circumstances could create, was the fact that they hadn't been in a room together for five years. I stood back a little to give them some space, and to let them hold each other for as long as they wanted. These circumstances were pretty severe but they both handled it well, and we were soon sitting, talking and drinking soft drinks as though we'd seen each other yesterday. We talked mainly about the progress of the Treaty and John's Pardon application, which I was still deeply involved in pursuing, as well as sharing family news from home and working out what John needed while we were there in Bangkok.

I had dreaded this reunion, knowing it was necessary but so hard for both of them, but thankfully Mum didn't go to pieces and managed to rein herself in so she was just a bit teary. John, too, was fighting to keep himself together. They both did their best to hide their real emotions. I guess they were staying strong for each other. I remember thinking that no mother should ever have to see her child in these circumstances. I know that's why John had always asked me not to bring her to the prison, as he was worried about how she would cope and didn't want her to see how he was living in Klong Prem. It must have been so hard for him too.

We managed to get all the food we had brought into him, which was fantastic, though after twenty minutes guards came around with the food in black bin bags and to my dismay everything had been piled in willy nilly without a care to the contents. I remember sighing as I noticed the loaves of bread squashed at the bottom. All too soon our hour with John had flown by, but saying goodbye was relatively easy as we knew we would be back the next day. Mum left with a shopping list from John, and I was so proud of the way she handled the situation.

During this visit, we were very touched by a group of Thai children sitting near us, who had travelled overnight to see their elderly sick father in prison. All they could afford to buy him was a few cartons of soy milk and a roll of toilet tissue, and when we noticed that they had no food or drink we offered them the vouchers we had for refreshments. Their predicament moved us to tears. They were very hesitant to accept anything from us until a prison guard explained to them it was okay. We also gave them packets of John's lollies to eat as it dawned on us how lucky John was to have so much. Their gratitude was overwhelming. Mum gave the eldest girl, who was about 14 years old, the Baht equivalent of about AU$40. When it was time for their father to leave, the children were sobbing uncontrollably. It was heartbreaking to watch, and Mum and I hugged them, trying hopelessly to ease their pain. Undoubtedly we would never see these kids again, but what a profound impression they made on us.

It hammered home the message that there really were some desperate situations here in Thailand, far, far worse than we could possibly imagine, and that we simply had to do whatever we could to help. John was our primary focus, but it was impossible not to feel for these people surrounding us every day. We would be going back to our luxury hotel, and then back to Australia, and even John would eventually get out, but these people seemed locked in a poverty trap from which there was no escape. It was so sad to see, and it really opened my eyes.

After visiting time was over, the inmates were instructed to line up and then sit cross-legged in rows on the floor, before they filed off to their cells. John was shaking his head and smiling, looking back at Mum and I with the children, wondering what on earth we were up to. I suppose it would have been a rare sight, as inside the prison it really is every man for himself, with sympathy for others very thin on the ground. This was by far the most emotional day for us on that trip, and one that made us realise that our situation certainly wasn't the most desperate. As we travelled back to the hotel we counted our blessings, trying to fathom how anyone could survive in that prison without family support. The cheerless truth was that many prisoners had no family or Embassy support and were left to their own devices. Just thinking of this really upset me and I fervently wished we could help in some way. Thoughts and ideas were starting to take root inside my head; I wanted to help those people who needed it the most.

We left the prison emotionally drained, hot and sweaty, but as we taxied back to the hotel I felt a great sense of relief that the reunion between Mum and John had gone so well and Mum had coped so admirably with the conditions of the prison. It was a great relief to get that first visit out of the way. I felt that Mum now knew what to expect and I could stop worrying about her. When we got back to the hotel, we showered and changed (as you seem to need to do more than once a day, just to feel slightly fresh in the humidity) before we decided to hit the streets. As with my first visit, I felt it was important to get out and do something else other than worry about John in the prison. Otherwise, we would have been overwhelmed by worry and grief, and we both knew that that would do John no good. We made a conscious decision to immerse ourselves in some serious relaxation therapy, to keep our minds from dwelling on what we had just witnessed so we could show up for John the next day looking upbeat and hopeful of a positive outcome. We flaked out for a quick nap that afternoon, before spending a quiet night in the hotel lobby bar, listening to the resident Filipino band.

The next day, Mum and I went downstairs for an early breakfast before setting out by taxi to Klong Prem. We waited for almost two hours to see John, and our spirits were deflated when we only were permitted a twenty minute non-contact visit through sets of bars and mesh. These non-contact visits really reinforce the zoo-like conditions in which the inmates are kept. The prisoners stand behind one screen of wire mesh, and visitors stand behind a second screen, set about ten feet from the first. The visits involve two swarms of people, the visitors and the inmates, all shouting through the wire mesh, hoping in vain for their words to be heard over everyone else. It is like trying to conduct a conversation across a major intersection during rush-hour traffic. With the cacophony of at least another hundred inmates and visitors yelling to one another in different tongues, it was almost impossible to have a conversation. Yet again, I was struck by the inhumanity of the prison conditions.

When we left and moved outside the prison, I phoned Dr John from the telephone box nearby, and he came out and asked us to come into a small office inside. He was a small, slim man with a very gentle presence. He was wearing a grey safari suit, and I think the fact that he wasn't in prison uniform immediately made him seem more sympathetic. I had found the prison guards to be so intimidating, in their tight-fitting khaki uniforms with their batons swinging as they walked, and the way their mirrored sunglasses hid their eyes, which gave you the feeling that you were constantly being watched. Faceless, anonymous, and imbued with a careless brutality, they would sit in groups throughout the prison, idly smoking cigarettes. For about twenty minutes, Mum and I sat with Dr John, talking about our John and the state of his health. Dr John was very helpful and reassured us that John was being treated for his tuberculosis, and that the treatment he was receiving was recommended by the World Health Organisation, which was comforting to know.

My constant harassment of the Embassy and anybody who could help me in any way escalated during my visit. I felt that actually being in the area meant there was no time like the present to try to sort things out. I set out to find out more about how things worked in Thailand. I was only beginning to understand that there was a huge amount of bureaucracy to contend with and that the important thing was never to make anybody feel like they could lose face by doing what you ask. Slowly but surely, I started to get to grips with how the system worked, but I knew I had a long way to go. On Thursday, we travelled into the city on a mission to get more information from various government departments.

Back at home, I had been making progress compiling John's Royal Pardon application, but it still seemed as though the Prisoner Transfer Treaty was worth pursuing. I had discovered that about twenty countries had an agreement with Thailand that enabled prisoners to serve their time in their own country. A treaty was looking more and more like a real option, beyond a Royal Pardon, and was a real ray of hope, so I was doing everything I could to revive the progress towards an Australia/Thailand agreement. I wanted to know why the agreement tabled in 1997 had never been passed, and I wanted to get it back on track. I was starting to realise that what I was doing could have serious political repercussions in Australia. It wasn't possible to get John home from Thailand under any present circumstances. So, I figured, in order to make it possible for John to get home, I would have to force the Australian government to sign an agreement with the Thai government to change those circumstances and make it possible. This would affect not just John, but countless others. Knowing this motivated me and drove me on.

Chris Hodges, an officer with the Australian Federal Attorney General's office, had told me that the tabled Australian Transfer Treaty might be based on an existing arrangement between Thailand and Germany, so prior to leaving Australia, I had contacted the German Embassy in Thailand and asked for a copy of their agreement. I had been advised to personally call in to the German Embassy to collect the document, when I next visited Bangkok. Traipsing through the city, Mum and I finally came to the Embassy security gates where we were greeted by a jovial Sikh man, who smiled at me and said, 'Mrs Singh, you must be my long-lost cousin from Australia!' After arriving, we waited a few minutes before the Embassy representative gave us the Treaty document. The Embassy staff were happy to provide it, but it was handed over with a word of warning. The Embassy officer stressed the very slow nature of the process and the fact that not many prisoners were successful in their transfer applications. This dampened my enthusiasm a little. We left the German Embassy and headed to our next appointment at the Australian Embassy, where we saw our old friend Roy. He asked for a copy of the German Treaty, which made me chuckle bitterly, as it seemed pretty obvious that I was doing a hell of lot more for the cause of Australian prisoners than the Australian Embassy. We then went on to meet with Embassy staff Kraisorn, and Peter Cantwell, and further discussed the possibility of putting the Treaty back on the Government agenda. Overall, the meeting was a very positive one and I felt certain that Roy had well and truly got the message that I would be constantly on his back wanting action on this.

The following day we had a contact visit with John, which was fantastic. I was heartened to observe that during the visit John came across as quite relaxed and much more focused; it was astonishing to note how quickly his spirits rose when family visits were taking place. We were over the moon to be able to get more food in to him, although the cheeky bugger complained that we hadn't brought enough Cherry Ripe bars! A sense of humour was a good sign.

Prison visits weren't allowed at the weekend, and that weekend was a long weekend in honour of the Thai Queen's birthday. We took the opportunity to rest, shop and generally get ourselves physically prepared for the week ahead. By this stage, Mum and I had become regulars in the hotel's cabaret bar. It was an oasis of sanity in the midst of a harrowing trip, where we could return momentarily to normality and even have a few laughs, something that was essential for our emotional well-being, but which under the circumstances I would have never thought possible. This trip with Mum was such a dramatic contrast to my previous visit a year earlier, when I certainly didn't have anything to laugh about, and had wandered around lost, not knowing what to do or where to turn.

On the holiday Monday, we had arranged to meet Sister Joan Evans in Klong Toey. We set out in an ancient taxi that hurtled down the Thai roads at an unsettling pace and I could see Mum's knuckles soon turn white from gripping onto the back seat. I gave the taxi driver Sister Joan's address on a small piece of cardboard and hoped for the best. After we had been on the road about ten minutes, a strange thing happened. I realised that our driver was rapidly slowing down—very worrying as we were in the middle lane of a four lane expressway! To our horror, he pulled up altogether, got out of the taxi and started to chase a piece of paper fluttering across the traffic-congested lanes. All the time dodging cars, he returned to the taxi with a proud smile. 'No worries madam!' he repeated three times, and then the penny dropped—the card with Sister Joan's address had slipped through a hole near the gearbox onto the road, and he had stopped the taxi to retrieve it. At the time, the experience was utterly terrifying, although now it's easy to see the funny side.

We arrived a little shaken but in one piece, only to find that the cab driver from hell was the least of our concerns. To our dismay, we realised that I had got the date wrong and we were a day early! We walked up the street in Klong Toey, and were shocked at the poverty we saw. Once again, I felt my eyes were being truly opened. This was like nothing I had ever seen before. The poverty was just overwhelming. It was obvious that this was the side of Bangkok the tourists were not supposed to see. We walked past run-down houses and shop fronts with windows boarded up, and small gatherings of men squatting by the side of the road playing cards and smoking like chimneys. We trudged through a maze of narrow tracks dotted with small food stalls, but the only customers looked to be the local dogs waiting patiently for scraps. It was hot and dusty, but the children wandered around aimlessly in their bare feet, almost care free, because this was all they had ever known. Here, there were people who literally had nothing. If something happened to you here; if you fell sick, there was nowhere to turn and nobody to help. Whole families lived in squalid, cramped conditions far worse than anything I had ever imagined. In the distance across a car park full of trucks, ramshackle huts had been built out of corrugated iron and cardboard in a vain attempt to keep the weather out. Three generations would have to live like this, and seeing a large family huddled under their shelter moved me to tears. I now understood why Sister Joan chose to live and work in Klong Toey. The locals had been neglected for generations, their poverty ignored. Given no chance to gain an education or improve their lot, the vicious circle of despair had continued.

We stood there wondering what in the world we'd do, when, strangely, out of nowhere, we were approached by a middle aged, well-dressed Thai man who offered to help us. This was not altogether surprising, as Mum and I looked extremely out of place strolling through one of the slum districts of Bangkok; this place was definitely not on the tourist map. We explained to him the reasons why we had ended up in Klong Toey and he was very touched at the thought that foreigners would want to visit the Thai poor. He asked us where we might want to go and offered us a lift, leading us to his car. In yet another wonderful and fortuitous twist to our trip, our rescuer promptly instructed his driver to take us to Pratunam Market and wished us a good day. At a moment in our lives when the worst side of human nature was omnipresent and could have been overwhelming, little Godsends like this were a constant reminder of the shades of grey in human nature, and the huge potential for good in this world. Meeting so many kind people who extended their hand to help without thinking made this journey one that I cherished so deeply.

On Tuesday, we set out after breakfast for the prison. In the week or so we had been at the hotel we had become part of the local fabric. The taxi drivers waiting outside the hotel greeted us with an affirmative 'Klong Prem' before we had a chance to tell them our destination. One elderly taxi driver told us that his son was also inside and that he had been left to care for his grandchildren as a result. Once again it was a telling reminder that the families on the outside sometimes suffer as much as the prisoners.

At the prison, while we waited for about an hour to get in, we chatted to a Dutch missionary who told us that she travelled to Thailand a few times every year to visit the prisons. I had no idea this sort of thing happened — that people from other countries and walks of life gave up their holiday time to care for those who had no one else. I felt heartened that there were people like this in the world, and as we chatted she seemed curious about which prisoner we were visiting. She was definitely more interested in the African prisoners and I thought how nice it was that she was dedicated to the inmates who seemed the worst off of all. I had noticed the high population of Africans in Klong Prem, with many from countries such as Nigeria and Uganda who had very little embassy or family support. These pour souls were in an even worse situation than our John, and in my naivete it took a little while to work out that one of the reasons why the Africans were so attractive to the missionaries was their willingness to convert to Christianity in return for practical support, such as food and money. Later I discovered that the deception worked two ways—there was a racket going on inside the prison where you could buy photocopied chapters from the bible and the prisoners would remember passages and recite them, thus conning the missionaries in return. Desperate times call for desperate measures, I suppose.

This was another non-contact visit in what we had dubbed 'the chook pen', due to the screens of wire mesh that separated visitors from the inmates. Our visits were already starting to take effect on my brother's spirits—John was bright as a button and never stopped talking about Liverpool Football Club, which was great to see. Standing next to him was an Australian prisoner receiving a visit from his Thai girlfriend. He was a tall, handsome and well-built fellow who certainly didn't look like a typical inmate of the Bangkok Hilton. His name was Mick, and like most of the other foreigner prisoners, he was in on a drug charge. John's reed-thin frame and general look of ill-health made him seem such a pathetic figure next to him. His thinness and unkemptness strongly contrasted against a tanned and vigorous man in good physical shape. The vast difference in their condition was largely due to the fact that Mick had worked out how to negotiate the prison system and whose back to scratch. He was in with the guards, and as a result was living a far more comfortable life than our John. Mick and I struck up a conversation—he was very warm and friendly and congratulated me for doing a media story about the prisoners' plight earlier that year. His mother, who lived in Sydney, had mailed him the first article I had done with Ruth Callaghan. Mum chatted with John whilst I tried to learn more from Mick about the chances of John being moved to a better building, one with more sleeping space.

Mick's Thai girlfriend, Muna, was visiting him so I apologised for taking up his time, as I know how precious these visits are to loved ones and how quickly time slips away. Muna seemed like a lovely girl and her English was perfect. We exchanged phone numbers and she offered to help us in any way she could. Having someone who could translate on our behalf would soon prove itself to be the answer to one of our many prayers—particularly one in relation to John's son Jason. I would soon learn that John had kept other secrets.

— CHAPTER FOUR —

It's fair to say that when we first got the news from John that my parents had a grandson and I had a nephew we never knew existed, it came as a shock. By that stage, Jason was three months old, but John's letter had not given us any indication of where his son was living, or even who or where the mother was.

John eventually told the story to us. He was arrested and imprisoned when his girlfriend Lek was pregnant, so she was left with no choice other than to return to her home village in North-East Thailand to have the baby. After Jason was born, Lek returned to Bangkok and visited John in prison.

John first set eyes on his son during a court appearance in February 1998. Not long after this, he was sentenced to ten years in prison and, as a result, Lek was left with Jason, no money, no job and no future for her and her children; Jason and three children from a previous marriage. From my perspective, what was so frustrating was John's refusal to inform us about Lek's circumstances. If we had known, we could have given her the financial and emotional support she so desperately needed when John was imprisoned. But as it was, left with little choice, she returned to the village and left Jason in the care of extended family, as her own father treated her very harshly and her mother had passed away some years earlier.

I would soon learn that Lek had set off to Bangkok to find work; she had previously worked in a sewing factory but this time thought she would try her luck in the bars. Although she kept in contact with John, the visits were few and far between. She needed to think of herself and the future of her children. Working and sending money back to her village was her priority.

Lek had sent John photos of Jason, and on my first trip to Bangkok I was able to see what my nephew looked like for the first time. I was totally smitten by this little boy and it was fixed in my mind that one day I would meet him and, better still, reunite my brother with his son. This would be my second mission.

We had no reason to think Jason was not being well cared for by Lek's family, but I often wondered what the future held for him in impoverished North-East Thailand. In between my first trip and this one, I received a letter from John telling me that Lek had met an American man, and he had asked to marry her and take her to the United States. John naturally was very upset by this news, but it was not clear from her letter whether or not she intended to take Jason with her.

Months had passed and John had heard no more. I had some phone numbers John had given to me, and I tried calling many times, but as I did not speak Thai and they did not understand English, it was a pointless exercise. So meeting Mick's girlfriend was like gold, as it provided a solution to this conundrum. I explained to Muna that John had a son living in North-East Thailand and we needed to make contact with his carers, but the language problem had prevented us from getting in touch on that trip. Time was running out and we were due to fly home in the next few days. We didn't intend to go to see Jason on this trip, as the village in which he lived was a twelve hour drive north-east of Bangkok, but we did hope to make contact with his carers and get more information about Jason's welfare. We also wanted to send them money, clothing and toys for Jason while we were in Bangkok. Muna promised to help us make contact with Jason's family, and we floated away from the prison on a wonderful high, with so much achieved. It's amazing how a day can change for the good or bad, all down to chance.

The next morning we set out again to Klong Prem, but without much confidence that we would be able to get a visit with John. After we told the taxi driver our destination, he asked us if we worked for an embassy. I explained our story to him; he also spoke perfect English and somehow did not fit into the mould of a typical Bangkok taxi driver. It turned out that he used to be a successful businessman, but had started driving taxis after the 1997 Asian stock market crash. He told us his uncle was a high-ranking officer at the special remand prison and offered to arrange a meeting with him. Although a little cautious initially, I said to Mum, 'Sod it! You never know, this guy might be able to help us,' and we decided not to look a gift horse in the mouth, and to take him up on his offer. The special remand prison was about two kilometres past Klong Prem, and on arriving there we waited in the taxi while our driver went inside. A few minutes later he returned with a middle-aged man dressed in full uniform, looking every bit the general. He greeted us with a smile, which was encouraging, and as he did not speak English, his nephew translated our story.

We followed him to his modest house just outside the prison, where his wife gave us a glass of water, and we wrote down John's name and building number on a piece of paper for him. Within a few minutes we were back in the taxi, thanking this caring fellow for his help and exchanging contact details, while he told us that if we thought there was anything he could do, to just get in contact. Although we were unsure if anything would come from this, we were still touched by another act of kindness from a total stranger. We tried to give him a big tip but he wasn't having any of it and firmly refused to take anything but the fare. In a country where everything, even kindness, can come at a price, this really stood out as an act of generosity.

We arrived into Klong Prem where, thanks to Mr Somphon, we were granted a non-contact visit, although we had to show our airline tickets to prove we were leaving for Australia the next day. It was a very nervous 15 minutes but we were soon making our way to the 'chook pen'. We managed to get into the lawyers' area, which was far quieter than the normal area reserved for non-contact visits. John continued to buck up; he was freshly shaven, looked great and once again chattered non-stop. The thought of him doing well made me think it would make it a little easier to say goodbye this time. We were not looking forward to our final visit the next day, but knew we had to keep our chins up for John's sake. Before we left, we managed to give him copies of pictures of Jason, that we had processed the day before, which also boosted his spirits.

We went back to the hotel for a quick shower before once again heading for Klong Toey to meet Sister Joan. She was waiting for us at the Old Mercy Centre and it was so lovely to finally meet such an extraordinary woman. Unlike the nuns I remembered from my convent school days, Sister Joan wore a calf-length skirt and a floral blouse. We had no need to feel nervous, as she was so endearing from the outset. She gave both Mum and I a warm hug. At the Centre, we met many children and took heaps of photographs. We then moved on to the New Centre, which housed the school and a hospital. The most touching thing was meeting the children with HIV-Aids. They were so beautiful and fragile looking, and I was deeply touched by their plight.

Then Sister Joan told me that she had a friend she wanted me to meet, and made a phone call to arrange it. She called her friend and within an hour we were introduced to Yvonne Ziegler, a tall blonde lady with a Birmingham accent and a very warm and down to earth character. The best was yet to come. Sister Joan was leaving it to Yvonne to tell us that her new job at the Australian Embassy was as Prison Liaison Officer. I could not believe our luck! Yvonne already knew John and she visited the prisoners once a month. We immediately hit it off and Mum and I knew that from that day things had changed for ever—this was a woman who saw John on a regular basis. Meeting her opened up a new world of communication between John and us, with regular reports that we knew we could trust. Needless to say, we felt like we hit the jackpot that day and could barely contain our excitement until we were on our way back to our hotel.

Meeting Sister Joan would change the course of my trips to Bangkok, and I felt I now had tangible support outside of the Embassy officialdom. Sister Joan is a major character in this chapter of my life, and has come to be someone whom I count as a close friend. Her comforting, but more importantly, inspirational presence beside me while I campaigned for John gave me much needed strength and enabled me to contribute a tiny sliver to the awesome task she has set for herself. It was not difficult to decide to fundraise for her projects and to be honest, there is definitely a self-serving component to this, for many times during the years to follow, it was immersing myself in her cause that held me together when the rest of the world seemed to crumble around me. Spending time with her when I was in Bangkok would ultimately become an uplifting experience, and one that provided a window into a world to which I would have otherwise been oblivious. Without her I would never have experienced seeing what real poverty is and how HIV-Aids destroys families. In the Bangkok prisons, I have seen what I once believed were the worst extremes imaginable—of sorrow, hurt and hopelessness—but I was wrong. Nothing touches me more than the daily triumphs and tragedies of Sister Joan's life in the slums of Bangkok.

On our last day in Bangkok, Mum and I got up early and packed our bags before setting out on our final prison visit before our afternoon flight. After such a wonderfully positive day before, the dread of saying goodbye was lessened by the knowledge that Yvonne would be keeping in touch, and that John was in the good hands of Dr John. We only had a half hour non-contact visit in the 'chook pen' but we still managed to have a good chat. I nagged John about his Pardon application and we discussed arranging some dental treatment for him. Despite being buoyed by our good fortune and success, saying goodbye was always a nightmare, and I was relieved when it was over. Thankfully, we had no time to ponder how John would fare without us as we needed to rush back to the hotel and grab our luggage before heading to the airport.

So many incredible things happened in those few days; it was such a stark contrast to my previous trip. My first experience in Bangkok had meant that I hadn't really wanted my mother to come with me and go through all the traumatic experiences, but having her with me had proven to be the best thing that could have happened. I felt that the barriers I had put up between us in order to protect her from the worst of John's situation were now down, and I could share more with her and be more honest. I knew in my heart that I would be back soon.

— CHAPTER FIVE —

It was wonderful to be back home. I had really missed Richard and my boys. I was worried that my spending so much time and energy on my brother, locked up so far away, would have an effect on my kids and my husband, but I kept reminding myself that John was family too, and I would have done this for any one of my own family. Hopefully they would understand.

Returning to work was much harder this time around as I had decided I needed to throw all my energy into getting the Thai-Australian Treaty passed. My daily routine had changed dramatically and I found myself talking to government bureaucrats, mainly in Canberra, all of the time. Richard would constantly get out of bed to find me burning the midnight oil, scouring the Internet for any information I could find about the relevant legislation. To my surprise, my previously nonexistent typing skills improved dramatically, but the downside to all this was that my monthly telephone bills cost the same as my mortgage.

Much of my research focused on the Thai Corrections Department website, which encouraged other governments to embark on prisoner exchange treaties. The Thai government were keen to do this for financial reasons. As treaties were already in place with twenty other countries, my question was—why not Australia? I started to phone every state department I thought could help or give me information, asking if they planned to do something to move the motion of a treaty along. Some people were more helpful than others but I was undeterred, and kept at it until I was pretty sure every state department would recognise my voice on the other end of the line, and would know exactly why I was ringing. I hoped this would spur them into action, if only to shut me up.

One person I was constantly in touch with was Chris Hodges, from the Federal Attorney General's office. It was his job to set up the red tape and endless legal documentation that at the end of the day would be passed through not only Federal parliament but also all the individual state parliaments, so once I got hold of his contact details I kept at him, harassing him and bombarding him with questions and requests for updates. I never imagined it would take so long to pass something that was already more or less agreed upon in theory. Although I'm certain there were times when he heard my voice on the other end of the phone and thought, 'Not that bloody woman again', he always had time for me and briefed me on all the developments or setbacks, of which we had more than a few. I was told that the New South Wales and Northern Territory areas were particularly uncooperative, but I didn't understand why.

About this time, Chris put me in touch with Malcolm Penn, the Planning and Policy Officer for the West Australian government. From past experience, I had gathered that dealing with government departments is never easy, but I couldn't believe my luck. Malcolm was so supportive and very sympathetic about John's incarceration. Like Chris in Canberra, Malcolm seemed happy to answer my endless questions and kept me up to speed with any developments.

It's well known that the wheels of bureaucracy turn very slowly. The weeks turned into months and I would often feel like I was getting absolutely nowhere. Inside, I felt that the urgency of what I was attempting to do was so keen, and when it seemed that no one was hearing the drum I was endlessly beating, I felt incredibly disheartened. It was so frustrating, and this seriously affected my private life. Trying to keep my business going became a real chore; although it was still very successful, my heart was no longer in it. I felt that at every available moment I needed to be at home, phoning, e-mailing and generally making a nuisance of myself to whoever would listen to me.

My parents and brothers, out of concern, tried to pull me back, and kept saying things like, 'What about your own family?' but at the end of the day they knew there was no stopping me. This was something I had to do and they had to accept that.

One morning I was ready for work and preparing to take the boys to school, when I heard on the radio that Paul Murray of *6PR* was having the Australian Prime

Minister as a guest on his talkback radio show. The news sent my mind racing, and it seemed a not-to-be-missed opportunity to talk to him about the Prisoner Transfer Treaty and personally highlight to him my brother's plight. I frantically delivered my boys to school, then dashed home and called my friend Jenny, who ran the hair salon next to my boutique. I asked her to put a note on my shop door letting the customers know that I would be late, explaining to her that I had a date with the Prime Minister. No doubt she thought I'd gone completely mad. Shaking like a leaf, I dialled the phone number and got through first time. I explained my reason for calling and to my amazement they were happy for me to talk to the Prime Minister. By the time they called me back, I had a million and one things zinging through my head. Here goes, I thought. Paul Murray had been giving John Howard a hard time about rising petrol prices immediately beforehand, so after wishing the Prime Minister a good morning, I reassured him that I wasn't on his case about the fuel situation. He laughed and then I launched straight into what I had to do, asking him when the Prisoner Transfer Treaty between Thailand and Australia would be ratified. I also provided him with a brief account of John's crime and the ten-year penalty. He was sympathetic and advised me that to his knowledge, the process was moving along and was now in the hands of the States and Territories approving the terms and conditions. He also asked for my details and said he would have the appropriate office contact me.

Although that never happened, I felt energised and excited by my boldness. Here I was, talking to the Prime Minister of Australia. What a cheek! I thought, but this was a new beginning. Going public seemed the only way to put more pressure on the government to move things along. More than anything, I wanted John out of that hellhole and even though he would have to serve time in an Australian prison, at least we would be able to visit him regularly and he would receive first class medical treatment. The prison doctor, John Lerwitworapong, worked miracles with what he had, but I would always feel better knowing John could get first-rate medical care in Australia.

Despite it being a bit of a fluke, my contact with the Prime Minister had not gone unnoticed. I felt more confident when phoning the DFAT and the Embassy, because I felt like I had gone to the top of the pile and been listened to, so the rest of them had better sit up and take note. I was now determined.

A few days after the radio show, I was on the phone to the Australian Consul in Bangkok and with tongue firmly in cheek I mentioned that I had been speaking to John Howard on national radio. I was met with a short, sharp, 'I heard.' Word travels fast when you get to the people who matter. I had got on with the consul Roy in the early days, but I detected a frostiness in his voice when I called him these days. I suppose Roy was just overwhelmed by work, and I didn't help matters.

John was never a great correspondent, but even in the absence of any letters from him, my mother and I kept up a steady stream of parcels and letters. I was regularly updating him with regard to the Treaty's progress and each of my letters always contained a paragraph nagging him to do some writing of his own towards his Royal Pardon application. This was an ongoing battle, as he would always sound so negative about the whole situation, and it was a constant struggle to keep him mentally afloat. This got worse as the weeks and months since our last visit went by. Yvonne saw him on a monthly basis and she reported that most of the time he would have little to say, although one thing stood out: his very dry Scouse sense of humour was still intact. Having the regular contact with Yvonne was a fantastic source of comfort.

I did at times become depressed with the slowness of the whole thing and the lack of enthusiasm on John's part. He just didn't seem to believe that anything could be done, and I was constantly facing an uphill battle with bureaucrats and politicians to get a move on. However, instead of just wallowing in that depression I started to look at what I could do to help others in Klong Prem too. I kept a look out for anything I could do, and investigated ways of easing the sentence for those prisoners who had nothing. This helped me through the frustrating first two years when it seemed nobody was willing to do anything at more than a snail's pace.

In November 2000, as well as doing my best to keep my finger on the pulse regarding John's Pardon application and pushing for implementation of the Prisoner Transfer Treaty, I was frantically busy at work in my fashion boutique. Christmas was looming and it was the most profitable time of the year. John was constantly on my mind and although it had only been four months since I had last seen him, I felt a powerful need to visit him. As if answering my mental prayers, I received a letter from DFAT in Canberra informing me that Klong Prem prison were going to have family contact visits, defined as a two hour visit, only permitted once a year. When Richard came home from work that day, I asked him what he thought of the idea of the two of us going to Bangkok to see John. Prior to raising it with him, I had done my homework and found a very good deal for the travel and accommodation. We had also just had an unexpected financial windfall, so I knew he couldn't object on those grounds, so as far as I was concerned there was no way he could refuse.

Richard was sorely in need of a break, having just finished four years working on the mines in addition to taking the lion's share of looking after the kids when I had been so preoccupied. He agreed to my plan. The last thing to sort out was our boys. They had never been without both of us for more than one night. We arranged for them to be looked after between their sets of grandparents, and then it seemed we were on our way.

Over the previous months I had been e-mailing and phoning Dr John and in one of our conversations he had told me that the prison was in great need of spectacles. Many who didn't have the glasses they needed had nobody to fall back on, or even if they did, more often than not their family simply couldn't afford to buy them. Here in Perth, there is a wonderful organisation called

Optometry Aid Overseas. Remembering the words of Dr John, I met with the founder, David Stephens, and after hearing the plight of the prisoners, he agreed to donate a few hundred pairs of glasses. The glasses have their own special story. Donated by the general public, they are then sent to a maximum security men's prison in Perth. The inmates repair, clean and grade the spectacles, making them ready to be donated to worthy causes all around the world.

Elated that I could do something to help, I contacted Thai Airways and explained what we were planning to do, asking if they would be kind enough to allow us excess baggage in order to transport the spectacles. I was transferred to a lovely lady named Mandy Godfry, who gave her blessing for us to have the necessary 60kg excess baggage allowance, for which we were eternally grateful.

Everything seemed to be beautifully slotting into place, until later the same day when I received an e-mail from a contact in Bangkok informing us the family contact visits had been cancelled because of a recent attempted break out in a rural prison. The idea was to punish everybody for the transgression, and so the family visits had been struck off. I called DFAT in Canberra, who were initially unable to provide confirmation of this, as it seemed my contact had passed on the news before it had filtered down the official lines. To my dismay I received a return call a little later advising me that my contact was correct and the visits had indeed been cancelled.

I was devastated, to say the very least. We would not be able to sit with John and have a normal conversation, and what about all the food and goodies we planned to deliver? There was so much at stake, so when we recovered from the initial shock of the bad news, we pulled ourselves together and decided that nothing was going to stop us going to see him—even if it meant only visiting John in the 'chook pen'. On previous visits I had been able to buy John fresh food on a daily basis from the shop outside the prison, so once again we took a positive approach, thinking that even that much was worth it.

When our day of departure arrived, we had 110kg of goods to take to Bangkok, which of course included essentials for John. We certainly did not look anything like typical tourists boarding a plane to paradise, and weighed down with bags, we attracted many glares from other passengers at the check-in desk; I remember thinking; if only they knew the contents of our cases were going to the infamous Bangkok Hilton!

The flight enabled Richard and I to spend some quality time together. We had both been working so hard and he had been such a pillar of strength over the past two years since we had heard of John's incarceration. We relaxed, had a few drinks and watched the in-flight movie, feeling like a husband and wife for the first time in ages.

Arriving at Don Muang airport with all our luggage was always going to be interesting, as there was no way we were going to blend in as Australian tourists. Fortunately, Optometry Aid Abroad had given me a letter to explain the excessive amount of spectacles, to prevent the possibility of us being mistaken for importers attempting to avoid duty. On reaching customs, in my excitement,

I unthinkingly breezed through and raced ahead, not realising Richard had been stopped and quizzed by a hostile customs officer. After a few frantic moments, Richard shouted at me to come back. I showed the officer the letter and reeled off a spiel about Australians helping Thais. We were soon on our way, thank goodness.

Because we arrived on a Sunday night, I had specifically asked the Australian Embassy to fax the relevant documents we needed to visit John the next day. But after making enquiries at the hotel reception, it was evident that the papers had not arrived. I was livid, as it totally derailed our plans; we needed to leave at eight o'clock the next morning to get to the prison and the Embassy did not open until nine o'clock. I later found out that there had been an oversight at the Embassy that caused us to miss our first visit with John. Having travelled all the way from Australia, and with only six days in Thailand, this was extremely upsetting – it was bad enough for us, but it was worse for John, waiting to be called from his building, only to find that we were not there. This kind of clerical oversight caused unnecessary grief for all of us. It's not exactly rocket science, I remember thinking resentfully at the time, trying my best not to lose my cool. I ended up spending half the morning on the telephone, trying to find out what had happened, and then Richard and I bided our time for the rest of the day, exploring the area near the hotel.

We arrived at Klong Prem early the following morning. Richard and John hadn't previously met so it was an introduction in addition to a visit, and it was going to be interesting to see how they got on. Not surprisingly, John was looking thin and pale. He was happy to see us but a little shy at meeting Richard for the first time. When I explained our no-show the previous day, he said it did not surprise him, as his relationship with the current Embassy staff wasn't particularly comfortable since he'd gone over their heads on his health issues. We shared all the news from home and his news from the inside, and once again the clock beat us and the visit had to end. We said our familiar goodbyes and I left with a verbal list of to-dos—buying fresh foods like cooked chickens, cakes and fresh bread. Someone had stolen his towel a few months before, which meant he had been without one since, so I bought him a Liverpool towel as well. I always loved shopping for him, as I knew it was his lifeline to the outside world.

By this time in our lives, Richard had changed his job and had taken up a new career as a prison officer, so one can only imagine the stark contrast he experienced between the state of the art prison he worked in in Australia and the third world conditions at Klong Prem. Although he had put on a brave face and acted as normally as possible during our time with John, travelling back to the hotel, Richard was very quiet. I don't think he could get his head around the conditions the inmates were kept in, and seeing them first hand, with a family member involved, hit him for six. The shock never really went away. For me, it was always good to get back to the hotel, have a shower and find the coldest beer in town; I always found this therapeutic, and a way of recharging my batteries for the next day's visit to the prison. It was the only way I could get through it.

Previously, back in Australia I had been contacted by Geoff Thompson, the Bangkok-based *ABC* TV and radio correspondent who was keen to meet with me, and attempt to see John. Up until this point, apart from the interview with Ruth, I had been reluctant to involve the media, but it was fast becoming a necessary evil. I was learning all too quickly that without making noise publicly, no one was ever going to do anything about John's plight, and we needed to get positive publicity to pressure the politicians into getting their act together and legislating the Prisoner Transfer Treaty. Without some media agitation and public scrutiny, John would most likely serve his full sentence before the necessary legislation was passed.

During that visit I called Geoff from the hotel and we arranged to meet outside Klong Prem the next day. I was feeling nervous and worried, and hoped I was doing the right thing by John. Richard went for a walk and left Geoff to do a brief interview with me. I outlined John's story and the hopes we had for the future, which centred on either having him transferred back to Australia or being granted a Royal Pardon. We then moved into the prison area to register to visit John. I was worried Geoff might be refused entry and I did not want this to jeopardise Richard and my chances of seeing John, so we went our separate ways at the registration desk.

Richard and I breezed through as we were familiar faces by this stage. Unsure of what had become of Geoff, we moved to the visiting area where John was waiting for us. I explained to John about the journalist who might be coming, but he was not worried by the possibility of media attention and shrugged his shoulders in a carefree manner. After ten minutes or so had passed, a Thai guard came to John and told him his visitors had been granted permission to see him in the Embassy room—a room normally only used by foreign embassy personnel and the inmates they were visiting—and in addition to that, he had another visitor waiting for him there. This was unexpected, and feeling very confused, Richard and I obediently headed in the direction indicated by the guard. Within moments we were standing with John and Geoff Thompson, with no bars or mesh between us, just standing face to face and being offered water by the guard on duty. I could not believe our luck, and wondered what on earth Geoff had said or done to achieve this. John and I hugged, and still in disbelief we chattered about life on the inside while Geoff took notes. Geoff was very sympathetic towards John and left before Richard and I, so as to give us some privacy. The irony of it all was terrific. We had arrived in Bangkok unable to get a contact visit with John, but here we were, totally out of the blue, sitting next to him. This was undoubtedly another of those small miracles bestowed on us.

We met up with Geoff outside the prison to discuss the outcome of the visit. He wanted me to go public with the grievances I had with certain Embassy staff, but I decided that it was not in John's best interest to go down that path. It felt as though we were at a very sensitive time, particularly with regard to the Treaty, so criticising the powers above could be a step backwards and put at risk the relationships that I had started to build with the Canberra officials. We said our goodbyes and Geoff continued to report on the progress or frustrations of the Transfer Treaty over the next year or so, before he was posted to the Middle East. I still don't know what he did that day at the prison to get us a contact visit with John but I will never forget him for that. On returning to the hotel I called Yvonne to let her know about our incredible good luck. She too was astonished that we got our contact visit after all, and was overjoyed for us.

Once again time was flying by and we only had one more visit with John. Without an official contact visit, we hadn't had much luck getting all the food parcels we had brought over from Australia into the prison for him, so we settled for stocking him up with food from the prison shop. We also topped up his bank account, for although he received an interest free loan every two months from the Australian government, John was a smoker and everything inside the prison had a price tag. My only option was to leave John's large box of food with the Australian Embassy and hope they might fare better than me, and it did make it in to him eventually, thanks to Yvonne. As we made our way to the prison, that familiar feeling of sadness engulfed me. Richard sensed my unhappiness, but tried to keep things as normal as possible.

John's change in mood after a series of visits was again evident on this trip; his shyness during the first meeting with Richard was a very different story to this visit. He was very chirpy and I could see the dramatic difference in his mood as he told funny stories of the antics of fellow prisoners, and made fun of me in front of Richard. This was confirmation of the value of human contact and I was so happy that we had made the journey. We were able to walk away from the prison with the comforting thought that John knew he was loved and that even when we were back in Australia we would continue fighting for his freedom.

Once I knew that John realised he had our love and support, I was able to turn my attentions once more to the other prisoners who needed somebody to lean on, for whatever reason. We organised getting the glasses we had brought over with us into the prison, as well as medical equipment and a laptop kindly donated to Bang Kwang prison. I had learned that the plight of foreign and native prisoners in all of the Thai prisons were the same as they were in the Bangkok Hilton, and I was delighted to be able to help in any way I could. Friends of Julie Dabala, who visited the foreign inmates, would still be there after we left, so it was great to know that when we were gone there would be someone else there to carry on the work. This thought provided me with a much-needed distraction from worrying about John, by helping me help those who didn't have the support my brother had.

I know the donations we managed to make made a world of difference for some of the prisoners, and heard that they were eternally grateful. I had asked John to spread the word about the spectacles amongst the inmates and it was truly amazing what a difference it made. A lot of the guys who obtained the glasses hadn't been able to read for five or even ten years, and it was amazing to think that something so simple as a second-hand pair of spectacles could change someone's circumstances and dramatically increase their quality of life. One man had not read for ten years, simply because he could not afford to buy a pair of spectacles.

The next day, we had arranged to catch up with Sister Joan again. She joined us at our hotel for lunch and it was wonderful for Richard to meet this extraordinary lady who has changed the lives of so many people. Sister Joan said she would make sure the Embassy received John's box as it was Saturday and we had no way of getting it to him. After she had left, I had some phone calls to make. I had been thinking of ways to do some fundraising for Sister Joan's projects and came up with the idea of getting my hands on a Liverpool FC shirt signed by their international players. My best friend Pat from my school days back in Liverpool had a son, John, playing for the football club, so I made a mental note to call her and run my idea past her when I returned to Australia. I knew that it would surely raise a few thousand dollars for Sister Joan's cause, and this could make a significant difference. Later that evening, on our way to the airport, I shared my brainwave with Richard, whose response was to give me a knowing look that I had become used to over the past few years, as he said, 'Yes dear.'

—CHAPTER SIX—

After my last trip to Bangkok to see John, I was even more determined to push for the Treaty to be ratified and to have his Pardon application ready to be submitted. Also playing on my mind was the unforgettable people I had met inside and outside the prison in Thailand. Sister Joan, Yvonne, Julie, Dr John and all the inmates and visitors who offered advice where they could seemed like a blessing to me and helped me to believe there was a light at the end of the tunnel, that there was hope.

It had been another busy Christmas at my shop but I barely noticed. Inside my head, all I could think about was bringing John home. Going to work each day was becoming a chore and I started thinking about selling the business. Months before, someone had approached me about buying a partnership in the business. Now I thought this was a great idea. It would free up my time so I could be at home more, and I would still have a much-needed income. My joy turned to despair though when just before the partnership was formalised, the deal collapsed and I was left thousands of dollars in debt to creditors. I'd stocked the boutique up to the hilt thinking I'd have the money to pay the creditors the following month. This was the last straw for me; I was totally crushed and felt like I couldn't face the world anymore. Richard and I didn't know where to turn. We had hit rock bottom.

It was Richard's birthday that week and instead of buying him his usual carton of beer, my mum bought him some lotto tickets instead. I had come home from work demoralised, and gone straight to my bedroom, when Richard came in and asked what you get when you match five numbers and a bonus number. I barely acknowledged him, but slowly it dawned on me what he was asking and I shot up from the bed to see the ticket. It turned out we had won roughly AU$10,000, but waiting for the newsagent to open the next day to confirm it was one of the longest twelve hours of our lives. It was a godsend.

Over the next few weeks we managed to sort out our creditors, and then out of the blue I got a call from a woman named Maureen. She had been interested in buying the business before, but the timing had not been right for her. Now, she was ready for business. I desperately needed out and Maureen wanted to take over as soon as possible, which was another godsend. It was a great weight off my shoulders to move on from the business because my priorities had changed dramatically. I needed to be home for the kids and also to carry on the fight for John. I really felt like I needed to do something extra special to pay back the good fortune I had just experienced.

After having one of my chats with Dr John Lerwitworapong from Klong Prem, and recalling the success of the campaign for spectacles, he gave me the idea of collecting books of all descriptions for the inmates of his prison. Now that they were able to, we needed to provide them with something to read. Over 6,000 inmates had no library facilities, and I guessed reading would help to kill the boredom of unimaginable sentences inflicted on people within the Thai legal system. English books and novels were virtually non-existent in the prison. One night I was listening to the DJ Graeme Maybury on a local radio station. Graeme is a Christian minister so I felt he would be sympathetic towards the inmates in Thailand. His program helped local community causes so I thought I'd give his talkback show a call.

I explained why I was calling and went into the reasons for me going to Thailand, giving a brief summary of our John's situation. Graeme was very sympathetic and gave out my number to his listeners. Within two minutes my phone started ringing and it did not stop until 11.30 that evening. Offers of books and magazines, and an offer to collect them came in from all over Perth. *What incredibly generous people,* I thought. Over the next few weeks, Richard and I, with the help of a guy named Bernard collected over 1,000 books.

I sent Dr John an e-mail and he was overjoyed to know that so many people as far away as Australia were so thoughtful to his inmates. I was happy to do this, and to have achieved it. I just felt that any little thing that could make the lives of the prisoners in any way easier was worthwhile, because I had seen the difference it made in John.

I explained to Dr John that I would be bringing them over on my next visit to see John. We stored the books in our garage and over the next few weeks I sorted them into different categories. I then packed them into banana boxes and stored them. The boxes weighed between 5 and 15kg, so again I needed to contact Mandy at Thai Airways to grovel for a generous amount of excess baggage. As always, she agreed hands down.

I was lucky to have the support of so many people. It was amazing to think that some of these people I have still never met to this day. Optometry Aid had also been in contact offering a few hundred pairs of prescription spectacles for me to take to the prison. I was also invited into Casuarina Prison close to my home in Perth to meet the guys who help to make this project possible. It was a wonderful prison-to-prison project helping desperate people.

* * *

Preparing myself for this trip to see John was taking me in all different directions. Although John's needs were my first priority, it was also important for me to do what I could in my small way to help other inmates who did not having family and friends for support, and were in dire straits.

Richard was taking me to the airport; once again I looked a sight checking in. I had two suitcases, one brimming with spectacles, and four banana boxes of books destined for the prison.

Mandy from Thai Airways had notified the check-in desk and to my amazement the guy let me take all the goodies, amounting to 100kg! I could have given him a big kiss I was so relieved. The check-in guy explained the flight was half-empty so we were in luck.

Once again I was saying my goodbyes to my long-suffering husband, before I headed to the bar for my mandatory Cointreau on ice to calm my nerves. Even after all the previous trips I was still not a good flyer, and I guess I never will be.

Arriving at the Sofitel Hotel, the same smiling faces greeted me. This time I got a few strange looks checking into a four star hotel with a collection of banana boxes amongst my luggage. I chuckled to myself—if they only knew where the books and glasses were going—knowing full well I would let them know by the end of my stay. I found that Thais in general had little time and sympathy for inmates, so why this *farang* would want to help left most of them scratching their heads.

Although I knew my chances of getting a contact visit with John were almost non-existent I still held some hope that maybe Dr John could pull some strings for me. On the day of my first visit to the prison I got to see John through the mesh and bars for one hour, but to my surprise we were only three metres apart rather than the previous four. *What an improvement*, I thought. Unfortunately, they had also painted all the mesh bright blue, which meant although we could hear each other better we could not see each other as well, due to the glare of the paint. What a crazy situation! It was as if we on the outside were being punished in an indirect way, and I found it so frustrating. John was his normal quiet self on visit one, but I knew he would buck up as the days ticked on.

I told him about the books and glasses and asked him if any inmates in his room needed glasses. He said two Thai guys were desperate, because although they had a prescription, they would never have the money to buy any glasses.

I told John to get their prescriptions for the next day and I would search through the case of glasses I had back in the hotel room.

The next day I got the prescriptions and to my surprise I found two pairs of glasses to match their requirements. I was so excited and could not wait to get back to the prison the next day.

John went on to tell me that these guys had not been able to read for years. They were so grateful and wrote me two beautiful thank you letters, wearing their glasses of course!

I had called Dr John and we arranged to meet at the prison the next day. I had the case of spectacles and the boxes of books to donate to the prison. He arranged for the boxes to be brought to the prison via the chemist outside and he then came to meet me and escort me inside the hospital wing where he worked. His first question was to ask me if I would like to see John, and of course I wanted to yell out, 'Yes of course!' but I very politely said, 'If that's possible.' I could not believe my luck.

Dr John asked an officer to escort John to the hospital, and within ten minutes I was sitting in a room chatting to my brother, both of us laughing and shaking our heads in disbelief at being left alone.

Later that day I was having afternoon tea with Sister Joan Evans and Yvonne Ziegler at my hotel. It was lovely to catch up with these dear friends who had been such a fantastic support to me. I hardly took a breath telling them all my tales from the prison and they were amazed I got to see John and have a picture taken with him. I always remember Sister Joan telling me someone was looking after me, and I think I know who she means.

The day before I left for home I arranged to meet the Embassy staff, mainly to compare notes on the progress of John's Pardon application and his ongoing health issues. Although he was being treated for his T.B. he was still too thin and I was very worried about him. I know I was a thorn in the Consul Roy Clogston's side, but I had to keep John's plight fresh in his head. At this time it became clear that the Australian prisoners were a burden the Embassy could do without and in some ways I understood this, but maybe if a member of their family were in this predicament they might have been more understanding.

Once again it was good to get home to my family. My head was full of ideas and tactics on how I was going to keep the pressure on Canberra. I think the success of the spectacles and the books campaign gave me a much-needed boost to carry on, and I felt determined to make a difference, hopefully for my brother John, but also for the many others living in terrible conditions in the Thai prison system.

I was still very upset by the fact that there were so many people in prison in foreign jails who had nobody to care for them, nobody to visit. I saw in John what a difference it made to have someone there for him, to talk to and provide for him in his hour of need, and I wanted to help others feel the same sense of having somebody out there who cared about their welfare.

One day I happened to come across a list of British nationals in prison in Thailand, and I picked two names at random to write to. I wrote a brief letter to each guy and made up a post-pack comprising a T-shirt, writing materials and chewing gum. I sent them off in the post, not knowing if they would be received well or how the two guys would respond. A few weeks later, I unexpectedly received a lovely letter from one of them, a man called Trevor Lund, who, as I was to find out later, was quite a remarkable person.

Trevor's letter was delightful and full of thanks, and reading between the lines I sensed a very special person was behind it. Trevor was a British national who had been incarcerated in Klong Prem prison for seven and a half years. He had made an error of judgement, to say the least, and found himself looking down the barrel of a life sentence for trying to smuggle drugs out of Thailand.

Whilst in prison he has not only turned his life around but he has also helped hundreds of fellow inmates. I was told he was an inspiration to many.

The most amazing and inspiring thing about Trevor was that as a person who was in such dire straights, he could turn his very negative situation around and help so many other prisoners. He started to teach inmates how to write and speak English, and was teaching prisoners almost full time; it would be fair to say he taught hundreds of Thai prisoners English, thus helping them secure a better future on release from prison.

Trevor and I became pen pals. I wrote often after that and he became a great source of information. Thanks to him I was always in the know regarding the prison contact visits and on a few occasions I informed the Australian Embassy in Bangkok and DFAT in Canberra before they were told officially by the Thai authorities.

I decided that on my next trip to see John in Bangkok I would make the time to visit Trevor and maybe get a contact visit. However, because they were only allowed once a year I knew a lot of red tape was involved.

My friend Pat in the UK had delivered on my request and sent me a signed Liverpool FC shirt. She was more than happy to help. It was an amazing piece of sporting memorabilia that I knew would attract a lot of interest here in Australia with the ex-pat Scousers. Australian Craig Johnson's placement on the Liverpool team as winger had inspired a strong Australian following. It also helped that Liverpool had recently enjoyed an extremely successful season, winning five trophies.

For some reason the figure of AU$5,000 stuck in my mind as a reasonable sum to hope for, though I had no idea how much the shirt was worth. Whatever was raised would go a long way towards improving the lives of the kids in Sister Joan's care.

I contacted Torrance Mendez, a journalist at *The West Australian* newspaper who had been very supportive over John's plight, to ask if he might help me publicise the shirt. Torrance had also met Sister Joan in Bangkok so he was more than keen to help me out. After doing a bit of research, I felt the shirt should be framed so I enlisted the help of a guy from the local paper who did framing part time. He did an amazing job for cost price, seeing as all money raised was going to such a worthwhile charity. Sister Joan was back in Perth on her annual break, providing a perfect publicity opportunity. I suggested to her that we both be photographed with the masterpiece, with the photo to be published alongside a write-up by Torrance. At first she was a bit media shy but with an ounce of gentle persuasion she agreed. We arranged to meet later that week at the convent where she was staying and the picture was kindly taken by award-winning photographer Ron D'Raine. The next day the newspaper printed the picture and the story. The article generated a very positive response but unfortunately not the dollars I had hoped for.

Thus Plan B swung into action. Being part of a football mad household, I was used to spending Saturday nights listening to the radio relaying the football games being played in the UK. I remembered that the show host was from Liverpool, so I called him and he was more than happy to promote the sale of the shirt on his program that evening. He also said he would talk to a friend to see if we could promote it on his weekly football television show on Channel 31, the public access station in Perth. The following Thursday night, Richard and I were heading for the TV studio. Although I was nervous I knew we could not miss an opportunity like this. The program compere Graeme Withe introduced me and gave a brief outline of our fundraising story, before asking me a few questions, and within minutes it was over. On arriving back home, my eldest son Sean told me that a man named Bill had called and would call back soon. I was anxious, wondering whether or not the TV exposure had paid off, and what kind of offer this guy might make. The phone rang, my heart was racing, and in the happiest of coincidences, Bill made an offer of AU$5,000 for the framed shirt, and asked me to call him the following day at his place of work. I was flabbergasted and hoped it was not a hoax call.

That weekend I went to Bill's beachside home. He is a fellow Liverpudlian so we sat down with his son for a chat and a beer. I could not believe the generosity of this man—while we were talking about the football-playing boys in Sister Joan's Centre, he offered another AU$1,000 to buy them football kits (Liverpool ones of course!). Bill also advised me to write to Liverpool FC's newsletter and tell them about our fundraising story, although he wanted to remain anonymous. I did as he suggested and sent an e-mail to the newsletter. Within days I received a reply notifying me that my letter was the star letter of the week, and as a result I could look forward to receiving an autographed Liverpool football in the mail. Needless to say, I was overjoyed with so many positive things happening at once. When the ball arrived a month later, I wrote to Bill. Although I felt quite uncomfortable doing so, I shyly asked him if he might be interested in making a small donation to Sister Joan in exchange for the ball. Two weeks later a cheque for AU$2,000 arrived in the post, made out to Sister Joan. I called her, and anyone else who I thought would listen, as I was so excited. Once again we were over the moon and could not believe Bill's overwhelming generosity.

The next day I deposited the cheque into Sister Joan's account and Mum and I set to planning our next trip to see John. We had been informed that the prison would definitely be holding the yearly contact visit, and the thought of Mum and I sitting with John was so exciting.

Keeping my finger on the pulse regarding John being transferred was a full time job at this stage, and I liaised with Canberra on an almost daily basis. I had become very interested in the movements of Foreign Minister Alexander Downer and the Prime Minister and had the news channels and radio stations constantly playing in the background, much to my husband's annoyance. Downer had signed an agreement with his Thai counterpart in July, I was absolutely delighted to hear. In theory, both sides were open to the establishment of a prisoner transfer treaty. It was a milestone and the hard slog of the last year seemed to finally be paying off. I was so excited I called Downer's press secretary, not knowing I was calling his mobile number in Hanoi. He answered and was bemused by my calling from Australia, but was happy to confirm that within the last 15 minutes the agreement had been signed. Needless to say, the adrenaline was pumping and I felt we were on our way to achieving our goal. But there still remained so many obstacles to overcome. We desperately wanted John home for Christmas, but each day brought compounding frustration at how much bureaucracy and red tape we had to constantly battle against. Over the next few days I spoke with Chris Hodges who was there to outline the next process, and he always made it very clear that we had a long way to go. Looking back, I'm glad I didn't have a crystal ball, because very soon something happened that changed the world and understandably put all other considerations on the back foot.

It was on 11 September that the actions of a few people would murder, maim and destroy countless people's lives forever.

After the events of that tragic and terrible day, I realised that I was not the most important issue on the government's agenda. I still went about my daily e-mailing and calling but used my discretion regarding whom I needed to contact in Canberra.

September 2001 brought despair and disaster to the people of the US, and the world, and domestically Australia also had its own tribulations with the Tampa crisis, when 450 refugees were refused entry to Australia after they had been rescued from the Indian Ocean by a Norwegian ship called The Tampa. It was a humanitarian refugee crisis played out on a global stage. These were two major factors that caused our dreams for John's imminent homecoming to unravel. Our government and parliament were understandably preoccupied, and the final blow was our Prime Minister calling an election in late November, which meant it would be February 2002 before parliament would sit again. They do say that bad luck comes in threes, and I was ready to believe this. I was devastated but given there was no getting around it, all I could do was swallow my disappointment and stay positive for John, although I dreaded writing to him to tell him the bad news. The thought of having to wait for the politicians to return to Canberra in February 2002 was too much to bear. How could I tell John about this when he was barely holding on to hope?

I had put my heart and soul into getting John back to Australia and really felt like we were getting somewhere, and helping a lot of other people on the way. The carrot had been dangled in front of me so many times and I did feel like there was light at the end of the tunnel, especially with the signing of the agreement. But now, with so many setbacks, I just felt like hopping on a plane and flying over to Bangkok again. Yvonne mailed me with the details of the next prisoner contact visit in December, so Mum and I started to get the ball rolling for a trip then. She wanted to come back with me this time and I was happy to have her there. I had a feeling I might need her beside me. We still had many more boxes of books to take over for the inmates, as well as the consolation of the success of our fundraising for Sister Joan. But for me, most importantly, we were on a life-saving mission to see John. He would always be very down when we first met him, being quiet, distant and depressed, but after a daily dose of love and attention, not to mention Cherry Ripes, he would undergo an amazing transformation. He always seemed to reach inside himself and drag out his North of England sense of humour, and this is what I wanted to see. I wanted to make sure that my brother was still himself, still our John, and I wanted more than anything to be able to tell him that he would be home soon.

— CHAPTER SEVEN—

In November 2001, just when the world was steeling itself to start using air travel again, Mum and I made our fifth trip to Thailand, accompanied by Julie Dabala, who was again taking the chance to go and see prisoners who otherwise would not receive a single visit all year. We brought with us 110kg of books and clothing to donate to the prison and Sister Joan, and we had AU$5,000 in donations plus the money donated by Bill back in Perth lodged into an account. Bill wanted us to buy football kits for the boys who lived at the Human Development Foundation in the heart of the Klong Toey slum area. Up to seventy boys lived on the top floor of the building and when I saw the conditions in which they had to live and endure, I had made it yet another mission of mine to do something for them, to brighten their lives for even one day, by giving them something that would make them happy.

First, I had to turn my attention and focus to my ongoing campaign to get my brother freed or transferred to Australia before it was too late. The Treaty being signed would still be no guarantee that John would be released. He may not have been eligible, or chosen for either a Pardon or transfer, and he didn't seem to have the faith to apply for himself, so I knew I had to keep as up to date as I could. Once again I was haunting the Embassy with my constant questions and requests for regular updates.

On that trip we had two contact visits with John and tried to make sure he was ok. But it was always hard to tell at first, until he opened up and started to talk. We had to keep his hopes and his spirits up, and the contact visits helped do this enormously. We hoped that every time we visited, we would leave having let him know he was loved and that there were people looking out for him. I filled him in on the Treaty negotiations, but again he didn't seem too pushed with the possibility of getting out of Klong Prem. As far as he could see, he would believe that when they came with the keys.

Having written to Trevor Lund and receiving his letters in return, I wanted to meet the man who had turned his own dreadful circumstances around to become a valuable helper to others, by teaching his fellow inmates English. I had written to Trevor and mentioned my intentions of visiting him. He was very taken aback that I could even think of visiting him, knowing that I had so much on my plate while visiting John. Personally I felt it was a privilege for me to see this man in the flesh. Trevor had also voiced his concerns regarding how John would feel about me visiting someone else, and asked me to get John's blessing, which I did. John didn't seem to care.

Thank God the British Embassy had faxed all the necessary documentation to our hotel. I had a two hour visit with Trevor approved for the next day. Keeping in mind I did not know what he looked like, it was going to be a very strange but exciting experience.

Mum, Julie and I set out in a taxi to Klong Prem and planned how we were going to make our visit as positive and helpful as possible. Mum would see John, I would see Trevor, and Julie some fellow Aussies in the women's prison. I suggested this plan as I thought at the time it would be a good opportunity for John and Mum to have some special time alone. Once inside the prison I waited in line to enter the contact area. My heart was racing and I was sweating like a pig. I started to stride past the Thai visitors and the guards were not sure what to make of me. Finally walking into the visit area, I was faced with the sight of hundreds of prisoners and visitors, mainly Thais, and I felt overwhelmed. I was asked by the guard who I was here to see, and I said Trevor Lund, but when he asked me what he looked like and I said I didn't know, he laughed out load and started to tell the other guards in Thai.

I was feeling very awkward and useless, but then on cue, a short, slim, whiter than white guy was walking towards me calling my name. Trevor was all I thought he would be. He had so much life in him; the total opposite to our John. We chattered and drank Coke over the next few hours.

To say we had never met before did not matter; he was an amazing guy and I knew we would be friends for life. We were very similar people. One funny thing was that he had a bright red pair of baseball boots on, and only a day earlier I had bought a pair for myself in the market, not that I told him at the time.

We drew a lot of attention from guards and inmates; they all wanted to know who I was. Trevor was well known to all because of his teaching, and I could see he was well respected. We had a very enjoyable and useful meeting, and Trevor proved to be very helpful with the amount of advice he had. He advised me on so much and seemed to know the ins and outs of Thai bureaucracy very well. He would prove to be invaluable.

* * *

I wanted to bring Jason to Bangkok, as I felt seeing his son would be a huge boost to John's self-esteem and would bring a lot of positive energy. It might even allow John to see that there was something worth fighting for. However, even with the help of Muna, I was finding it really difficult to contact and talk to Jason's carers and another friend who had offered to help fell by the wayside. As a result, I was never quite sure if they understood what I was asking, if they were unwilling or unable to help. They lived a huge distance from Bangkok I knew, and would have had very little money to make the journey, and perhaps they didn't want John to have anything to do with Jason at all. I just didn't know, and not knowing was enormously frustrating.

I understood it was not the job of the Embassy to nursemaid the relatives of Australian prisoners, but I knew Kraisorn would help with the nod of his superiors, whom I had yet to meet. I needed to vent my frustrations, and had the perfect opportunity when I organised a visit to meet the new Consul Warren MacIlwain. He seemed nice enough over the telephone, but face to face meetings usually brought out the best and worst in these guys. Later that day Mum and I set out for the Embassy. I was really nervous because I knew I needed their help and time was running out to get Jason to Bangkok.

When we arrived we were made very welcome, and in five minutes I explained our situation to Warren. Without hesitation he called Kraisorn into his office and instructed him to make the much needed phone calls to Jason's family.

We would have to wait and see if they would come to Bangkok, but he said he would let us know as soon as he heard from them. This I felt was a huge step forward, and a huge improvement on previous Embassy interest in the case. While Kraisorn made the call I had a very good chat with Warren regarding John's health and it seemed that he was not impressed by the lack of cooperation John and I had experienced with some of the previous Embassy staff. Unlike his predecessors, Warren did take a lot of interest in the welfare of the Australian inmates. Kraisorn came back into the room but unfortunately the woman with whom he needed to speak was out working in the rice fields and would not be home until later that evening. Warren then instructed Kraisorn to call again that evening on his work mobile phone, to make sure he contacted her as promised.

Turning my attentions back to other matters to take my mind off John for a while, I shared my intentions about buying football kits for the boys at Klong Toey with Sister Joan and Yvonne. Yvonne very kindly offered to pick us up at the hotel with her driver and take us shopping for the kits. When we hit the streets, every shop was brimming with sporting goods of all types but mainly football gear. I approached the shop assistant and when I explained what I was looking for she was very enthusiastic to help. She worked out how many shirts and shorts we could buy for the equivalent of AU$1,000 and within minutes she was on her mobile phone calling her father's factory with the order. To my astonishment, she finished the call and turned to me, telling me that seventy full kits would be delivered to us within the hour. AU$1,000 wasn't that much to most Westerners, but it was a small fortune to most Thais.

We went for a walk to pass the time and on returning to the shop, a wonderful thing happened. The assistant confessed that she was embarrassed by the fact that we, as foreigners, were doing so much for her fellow Thais. This initial statement took me aback, and I was even more surprised, though pleasantly I must say, when she went on to donate a further forty football kits and about twenty high quality sweat shirts that she had in the shop. Mum and I were elated by her kindness and thanked her over and over again. We left the shop promising to come back one day, and started to fill up the boot of Yvonne's car with our booty.

As we were driving across town to see the boys, Yvonne's mobile phone rang. It was Kraisorn from the Embassy telling her that the family who were taking care of Jason would be arriving in Bangkok the next day and they would meet us at the Embassy.

It was a surreal situation; a dream come true. This was the news we had prayed for; I was so happy and excited I wanted to burst. Yvonne kept on repeating, 'Isn't it exciting!' This became her trademark comment over the next few years. Without the help of this new consul at the Embassy, I don't think it would have been possible to meet Jason's family, at least not as easily as we did. I felt like we were at last getting some breaks, and that the right people were in place to help us through this.

My brain was so full, but for a change it was overflowing with positive things. We arrived at the Human Development Foundation and Sister Joan was waiting for us. She shook her head in disbelief as we began unloading the car of the numerous boxes. The boys were still in school so we walked through the building chatting to younger children and anyone else who happened to be around. The building not only housed the boys but was also a school and a hospital mainly for HIV/AIDS patients with no family support. It was very emotional seeing these poor people facing certain death but with so much dignity. It also put our John's situation into perspective; there are so many people so much worse off than him through no fault of their own. At least John had the love and support of family.

Right: John and I in his first week with our family in Liverpool.

© *Barry Doran*

Below: John never carried much weight but I was horrified to see how thin he had become while in prison.

© *Ian Cugley / Sunday Times*

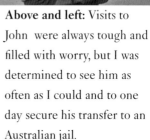

Above and left: Visits to John were always tough and filled with worry, but I was determined to see him as often as I could and to one day secure his transfer to an Australian jail.

© *Steve Sandford*

Below: Klong Prem prison, the notorious 'Bangkok Hilton' became a very familiar place for me over the years as I visited John and other inmates who had nobody else to turn to.

© *Ian Cugley / Sunday Times*

Right: I am proud to know Trevor Lund (middle runner), an inmate at Klong Prem who has turned his life around. He was the man behind the highly successful Bangkok marathon run within the grounds of the prison, which helped to raise funds for the poor of the city.

© *Steve Sandford*

Left: Sister Joan Evans does amazing work with the poorest of the poor in the orphanages and slums of Bangkok. She opened my eyes to a world I did not know existed, and has made me a better person for it. As my visits to Thailand to see John became more frequent, under Sister Joan's influence I became deeply involved in many campaigns to help those who needed it most.

© *Steve Sandford*

Bottom Left: I also campaigned to improve the conditions for the prisoners in Thai jails, and have continued to write and receive many letters from inmates and their families.

© *Frances Andrijich*

Above: I was completely overcome with emotion when finally, after years of campaigning, John was transferred back to Australia. My husband Richard and I so happy to have him back, but the happiness wasn't to last.
© *Ian Cugley / Sunday Times*

Below: John's son Jason, here sitting on Richard's shoulders, quickly adapted to l in Australia, and bonded with my sons. He has become one of the family.
© *Alf Sorbello*

Sister Joan called us upstairs when the boys started to arrive home from school. I've never seen so many smiling faces in one place, and they gathered around Sister Joan whom they all clearly loved dearly. The nun explained who we were and what we had bought for them, courtesy of a man named Bill in Australia. They were so excited and without hesitation started to try on the football gear. Julie and I were furiously snapping away with our cameras and the sea of smiling faces dressed in Liverpool-red would be a wonderful memory. We were leaving for Australia in two days so Yvonne and the football coach at the foundation said they would organise for the boys to play a football game the following week and send us the photographs, in order that Bill might see where his money was going to.

After all the excitement died down the boys were off to shower and have dinner, so we said our goodbyes and headed back to the hotel. We had a fantastic day and achieved so much, and I was so looking forward to a shower and a cold beer. Tomorrow was going to be another enormous day. Meeting Jason for the first time was going to be the icing on the cake for this trip to Bangkok.

* * *

Arriving at the Embassy the following afternoon, I was wracked with nerves but so pleased to see Yvonne's familiar face as she came down to the security gate and cleared our entry with the guards. She was beaming, saying, 'Wait till you see him! He's so cute.' On entering the room, Jason and four family members were sitting waiting for us, looking just as nervous as we did. Yvonne was right; Jason was so cute and Mum and I just wanted to give him a big hug, but we resisted, not wanting to frighten him, and tried to hold back our tears of joy.

He clung to a very kind-looking lady in her mid-fifties we later learned was Mere Luom. Her husband Boon Luom stood up and shook our hands and the younger couple in their twenties sat and smiled but looked too nervous to move.

Warren very kindly gave us the use of his office for about one hour and Kraisorn had his work cut out acting as our translator. It was a tense and awkward meeting, but I felt we got off to a good start and that we had all got on very well. There were so many questions I wanted to ask: Where was Jason's mother? How did they end up taking care of him? I was sure they had questions of their own. Most importantly, I wanted them to know how grateful we were to them for looking after Jason, and hopefully through Kraisorn I got this message across. I noticed that there was clearly a rock solid bond between Jason and Mere Luom, and I wondered if this would cause problems. I hoped it wouldn't, and couldn't help but imagine how difficult this all was for them. They looked after him every day, and suddenly, out of the blue, a woman they had never met before wants to meet him and bring him to a prison. All I could do was try to reassure them that I had Jason's best interests at heart. I wanted him to meet his father.

We arranged to meet the next day at our hotel and from there we would all head off to Klong Prem to see John. Outside the Embassy we said our goodbyes. In a fit of paranoia, I didn't want to let them out of my sight in case they never showed the next day. Although they were genuine, they also wanted to be heavily compensated for making the trip to Bangkok, which in a way was only fair. They didn't look like they had a lot of money to throw around. Mum and I had anticipated this. From the footbridge we were crossing I looked across and could see them from a distance, and it suddenly hit me how strange and yet wonderful this situation was. It was so unbelievable to think that in this busy Bangkok street stood my brother's son, my nephew, that endearing little boy we had only seen in photographs over the past few years. It was another miracle in this journey.

* * *

Feeling anxious as ever, Mum and I went to the supermarket to buy cakes and sandwiches for the family who were due to arrive at lunchtime. Kraisorn had promised to come along and translate for us, and as he arrived early, it gave me an opportunity to discuss issues that I would like him to translate to the family. Without him it would have been a nightmare. We had promised to pay the family's travel costs, but we also wanted to give them money for Jason's upkeep and education. I hated talking about money, but I knew it would be the most important thing on their minds.

To my great relief, Jason and his family did arrive at the hotel, on time and as promised, but to my surprise they had another family member with them, who they said was a taxi driver in Bangkok. He was very intimidating looking, complete with tattoos and missing front teeth. Mum and I had also been shopping for treats for Jason, buying gifts of toys, clothing, and anything else we thought he'd like, and they were strewn across the room, all wrapped in Christmas paper.

Sitting in the relatively luxurious hotel room probably made them very uncomfortable at first, but Jason was becoming very relaxed and that in turn settled everyone down.

He played happily with the toys we had bought him; but I couldn't wait to bring out a special present for him. Seeing as we were going to see John, or 'Papa John' as he was now being called, we thought it would be a great idea for him to wear a Liverpool football kit. Jason insisted on going into the bathroom to get changed, and when he finally appeared looking shy but endearingly cute, we all let out a cheer.

The family seemed more relaxed as they ate and drank with us. During our conversation they said Jason's mother Lek had taken him to America with her. They also claimed that she didn't support him financially, but we later found out that Lek actually had been in touch and was giving them financial support while they cared for Jason.

They continued, saying three months later Jason had returned to Thailand with his mother only to be left with other extended family members. What amazed us was that John and all of us back in Australia had no idea Jason had ever left Thailand. John would never have been able to see his son again had he stayed in America. For us, he would simply have disappeared without trace. We were shaking our heads in disbelief, thinking about what this little guy had been through. It made me more determined to fight for the future he deserved.

Jason was becoming much more approachable by the minute. He was so excited, ripping open the presents, and just like any other three-year-old child, he was only interested when the wrapping paper revealed toys. He instantly discarded the clothing. I asked Kraisorn to bring up the subject of money, to find out how much Jason's carers wanted to compensate them for making the 16 hour round trip. After a minute or so of discussion in Thai, Kraisorn and I left the room and he told me that the family had asked for ten thousand Baht, which was the equivalent of AU$500. I asked Kraisorn to translate the counter-offer Mum and I had devised: we would give AU$300 to the family, and set up a bank account for Jason's upbringing and education. They seemed more than happy with the result.

We all headed off to the prison, and once again my heart was in my mouth as they left separately with the burly, tattooed man. Once more, I wondered if we would see them again. I was worrying unnecessarily, as when we arrived they were waiting outside the prison for us. The next hurdle was to get them permission to see John. Although Mum and I had the necessary documentation for a contact visit with John, Jason and the family did not. It was too late to apply to the Corrections Department so I decided we would cross that bridge when we came to it, hoping the Foreign Affairs officer would take pity on this extraordinary situation and let them inside. It was in the hands of Kraisorn to explain the situation to Mr Somphon, the Thai officer whose expressionless face always left me wondering if he would put that much-needed 'permission granted' stamp on that piece of paper. Mr Somphon spoke to the family members one by one, and after taking down their details from their identity cards he stamped the papers and dismissed us with a now familiar nod.

Contact visits were always a very chaotic time for prison staff, not to mention the emotional roller coaster for visiting relatives, not only Thais but foreigners who come from all round the world for this special occasion. You are allowed to spend two, one-hour visits sitting with the prisoner and the visitor is allowed to take in fresh food so special treats like pizza and K.F.C. are always high on the list.

As we walked through the gates to the visiting area I wondered how John would handle the situation. The last time he had seen his son, Jason was a three month old baby, and now he was a lively three year old child. I saw him sitting and waiting with other Western inmates and he slowly stood up to greet us. I could see he felt very shy at meeting Jason and the Thai family, but fortunately John speaks fluent Thai, so they soon broke down the barriers. Boon Luom was trying to encourage

Jason to go to John but he refused. Seemingly relaxed, he stayed close to Mere Luom. After his initial shyness, John seemed to take it all in his stride. He was never one to show much emotion, and I couldn't believe how calm he was considering the circumstances. The Thai family were keen to ask him a million and one questions, so while they did that I went to buy soft drinks and to check that all the food we had sent into John was on its way.

Jason seemed oblivious to his surroundings; the Thai family were telling him about Papa John, but to a three-year-old it did not mean much.

John was talking to him in Thai, which was a sight I will never forget. However, it became clear that they didn't fully understand each other. Jason spoke Issan, which is Thai with a Laos dialect, because he had been brought up in North-East Thailand, near the Laos border. This hammered home to me just how much of a distance there was between them, and how much work needed to be done.

It was almost time to leave. In the heat and humidity we had all started to wilt, but as far as we were concerned it was worth every drop of sweat. Ever since we had received that first, life-changing letter from John I had dreamed of this day, and it proved that dreams do come true. I just hoped in my heart it would give John the boost he needed to stay strong and to focus on his future outside this God-forsaken place. He has a beautiful son, I kept telling myself: what more could anyone want?

The family told John they would visit him when they were next in Bangkok and Jason gave John a hug, still not fully comprehending that this was his papa. Outside the prison we thanked them for coming to see us and I stressed to them we would help with Jason in any way we could. Jason gave Mum and I a kiss and it was very hard to keep our emotions from getting the better of us. Tears welled in my eyes as I watched them drive away in a taxi, waving to us until they were out of sight. We had shared so many highs and lows, and this day was so full of mixed emotions we did not know whether to laugh or cry. As they disappeared into the distance, Mum and I simultaneously voiced the thought foremost in our minds: would we ever see Jason again?

the work of the Ombudsman. I had been involved

—CHAPTER EIGHT—

Returning to the normality of family life was always a challenge, but not having the huge burden of the shop on my shoulders made it easier. I was boosted mentally by the amount of positive things Mum and I had achieved during our last trip to Bangkok. Meeting Jason for the first time was well and truly a miracle I had long prayed for and I felt I needed to acknowledge the help of Warren, Yvonne and Kraisorn from the Australian Embassy. I'm certain that without their help we would not have achieved half of what we did.

I wrote a letter to the Australian Ambassador to Thailand, Miles Kupa, singing their praises, and also sent one to the Department of Foreign Affairs in Canberra. Dealing with the previous Embassy staff had become a very frustrating affair and instead of their assisting us, most of the time I felt like an unwelcome intruder asking too many questions. This had all changed when Warren took over.

I was still in regular correspondence with Dr John in Klong Prem hospital regarding John's ongoing health issues, and particularly his T.B. John had completed his six-month course of medication recommended by the World Health Organisation and issued free to the inmates, and although he was no longer experiencing the chronic coughing, fever and night sweats, he was still far too thin for his frame. T.B. is rife in Thai prisons but for a Westerner to have it was unusual. Then again, to me, the whole situation was unusual.

John did not have much faith in the prison staff or the third world conditions, but I knew Dr John was doing his best on a very small budget.

It was T.B. Awareness Day and I read with interest an article in our local newspaper about the Perth Chest Clinic. I called them and explained John's predicament.

The doctor I spoke to was very helpful and asked if Dr John could mail him a copy of John's latest x-ray. I was more than happy to do this, because if John was in need of further treatment I felt this would be confirmed with a second opinion. Dr John willingly obliged in sending the x-ray and I was delighted when the doctor at the chest clinic here in Perth told me that although John still had scarring on his lungs, there was no longer any sign of the T.B. This was a great relief and I immediately e-mailed Dr John and my brother to share the good news.

Yvonne would still see John at least once a month, so it was good to know he was receiving extra food, and Mum and I had topped up his prison account and left money with Yvonne to buy food for him.

One night in Bangkok, Yvonne and I had been for dinner and she remembered she had not bought shuttlecocks for an Australian inmate serving life in Bang Kwang prison.

Without a moan or a groan she paced up and down Silom Road at 9pm looking for real feather shuttlecocks. I couldn't help but think that this was far beyond the call of duty, but that was just Yvonne looking after her 'boys and girls', as she would refer to the Australian inmates.

I was still making my almost daily e-mails and phone calls to the relevant government departments in Canberra, trying desperately to harass them enough into making sure the Treaty with Thailand would be signed very soon, and that John's name would be top of the list when it was finalised. I was at this stage still working away non-stop on John's Pardon application after over two years of research and re-writes, but I had a horrible feeling it wasn't strong enough. I tried to stick to the examples of other applications, but it was really all over the place. I had sent a copy to the Bangkok Embassy so that Warren and Kraisorn could have a look at it. They confirmed my fears that it was a mess.

I had paid twice for it to be translated into Royal Thai, but both times I had been left unhappy with it, having paid out a few hundred dollars. The emphasis I placed on certain issues was getting lost in translation. I felt it very important that all documentation about John's T.B. and ongoing health problems should be highlighted in the application, so I called Warren and asked him to go through John's file to see what he could find, and more importantly, use.

Around this time, I had received a letter from John, and it crushed me to see that once again he seemed very down and depressed, so much so that for the first time I was very worried about his mental state. John also mentioned that the prison now banned the inmates from cooking on camping stoves, which meant he couldn't prepare his own food anymore, and had to rely on prison food he couldn't get used to. That letter broke my heart but it made me more determined to get him home as soon as possible. I voiced this to Warren and he said he would look into it when attending Klong Prem with the Canadian consul that week.

Meanwhile, I still felt like I had to do something to pay back all the good deeds that were being done to aid me in my campaign, and all the kindness shown to me in my hardest times. Since my husband had left his old job to become a prison officer, he was coming home every day with stories of the goings on in prison. At this time, the Indonesian crew from the Tampa crisis were being held in Rangeview Juvenile Detention Centre where he worked, and saddened by their conditions, I decided this would be a good chance to help some people in a very unfortunate position.

The Palapa, the wooden fishing boat rescued by the Tampa, had been crewed mainly by young, impoverished Indonesian boys, lured into this potentially deadly journey with the promise of US$100—a sum of money that would take them a year to earn fishing.

The crew deemed to be under the age of 18 were flown to Perth, where they were then detained to await trial on people-smuggling charges.

At this stage there were about eight boys, but some were undergoing tests to prove that they were over the age of 18. This meant they would be tried as adults and transferred to an adult maximum security prison in Perth.

In general, the boys were doing well. They had settled into the routine of their new surroundings, but cultural problems set in. They couldn't get used to the diet, they had a different religion, and they were missing their families. Many of the boys had not travelled outside their fishing village before. It was like a complete mirror image of what it seemed to be like for a Westerner in a South-East Asian jail, far away from home, surrounded by unfamiliar things, with nobody seeming to care. I had been determined to show my brother that this was not the case with him, that someone did care, and now I felt it was my duty to show these boys that they were not alone either.

One day Richard suggested to the boys that he would conduct a cooking class with them. The boys gave Richard a shopping list and the next day we set out to some Asian shops to locate suitable food. We managed to find all the ingredients and not only did the boys cook up a feast for themselves, they attracted the attention of most of the staff on duty that day too.

Although at this point I'd never met any of the boys, I felt as though I knew them, listening to Richard's tales each evening. I sympathised with the boys mainly because they were incarcerated in a strange country thousands of miles away from their families.

I asked Richard if it would be possible for me to visit some of them, and this was the start of great friendships that lasted till the boys were either found not guilty and deported, or guilty, and finished their sentences.

Aksal was the first boy I met. He was 17 but the authorities said he was 18. The funny thing was that on seeing this boy sitting in the visit room waiting for me, he looked not a day over 15. I could see he was nervous at meeting me and also suspicious as to why I would want to visit him. Also being the wife of a 'Sir', a guard's wife, was a little daunting for him. Aksal had one of those smiles that lit up a room and the kindest eyes I'd ever seen.

Thankfully his English was good so we managed to talk about many things, mainly his family and how much he missed them. I felt like I really connected with Aksal and hoped this would be the first of many visits. Unfortunately for him though, he was transferred to Hakea maximum-security prison not long after we first met.

I knew it would be tough for him being just a boy, mixing with some of the toughest criminals in West Australia. I promised him I would keep up the visits but I wasn't sure how I could do this. I met my good pal Julie for lunch one day and started talking about this, and between us we came up with the idea of working out a roster for visits. Julie had visited many inmates in Thailand so I knew she knew what to do, and would be a good visitor for the prisoners to have.

Another special boy was Henry; he was much quieter than Aksal and did not speak much English, but you could tell immediately that he really missed his family terribly. He worried me because he seemed unable to show his feelings, unlike the bubbly Aksal.

As time went on and Julie and I kept visiting, Henry seemed happier and we were always greeted with a smile. The boys participated in many classes including woodwork, and to my surprise after one visit Henry presented me with a coffee table and ashtray he had made. They take pride of place in our home today.

Although the Indonesian Consul in Australia had visited the boys in Perth, they still needed things to help them connect to their culture. We talked about getting Indonesian music and reading material together, but to be honest, I really didn't know what I was looking for, or where to look. I contacted an Indonesian Christian church in Perth and they were very happy to help. The minister asked his congregation to donate books and music tapes, and a few weeks later when I attended the service I was presented with two boxes of gifts to distribute to the boys and their friends.

They were overwhelmed by the generosity of the congregation and I know their lonely stay in prison was made more bearable by these acts of kindness.

The boys eventually returned to Indonesia in September 2002. They were so excited at the thought of seeing their families again. Richard and our twin sons Michael and Kieran came with me to the Immigration Detention Centre at Perth airport to say our good-byes to the boys. We did not realise they only had the clothes they were wearing, so the next day we went shopping and bought them warm tracksuits, and my eldest son

Sean had lots of things he'd outgrown. They thought all their Christmases had come at once. I will always cherish their friendship and hope one day to meet the boys again. Under different circumstances of course.

All of this helped to distract me from worrying about John for a while, but soon my fears began to grow again. With no word of the Treaty being ratified, I sensed John was becoming more and more despondent the longer he was locked up. He knew I was trying to help; he just didn't believe I could do anything for him.

Other issues soon came to the fore that I really hadn't wanted to face; the cost of my campaign was becoming a real problem and now that I was without a business, I was getting myself and my family further and further into debt. The mounting bills and anything else marked URGENT in red ink were left unopened and ignored for days on end. I had become so involved in trying to secure John's release or at least improve the conditions for him, the other inmates and the desperately poor of Bangkok, and getting the Treaty ratified, that I hadn't noticed how much trouble I was putting my family in financially. When I did finally realise, it came as a huge shock to me. At the time I just didn't see it, but looking back I guess I was shamelessly putting John's cause before absolutely everything else, and under the strain of this, my whole life —my family, my marriage, my own health—threatened to fall apart. My doctor had become worried about me as my stress levels went through the roof, and he prescribed Prozac, but I didn't feel like it did any good. The money worries suddenly overwhelmed me.

Making one or two trips to Thailand a year, which included a lot of spending money and charity donations, as well as the constant long-distance phonecalls, the internet research, and the loss of a steady income, added up to make one big financial disaster. In all, I must have spent well over AU$50,000. This was a big wake-up call, but I was still determined to see it through, and my blind determination and stubborn refusal to give up led to further strains on my personal life. I had felt guilty all along that my kids were missing out on holidays because of me, but it became clear that they were beginning to suffer from the turmoil, as was my husband, who quite rightly questioned my devotion to my brother, who didn't seem interested in being helped and never really realised how much time, money and effort I was putting into his campaign. All I knew was that I had to stand by John. He was my brother and I wasn't going to let him rot away in a foreign prison for what he had done. Not surprisingly, our relationship started to get a little bit messy, and but for Richard's amazing patience and support, we would have fallen apart. We had tough times, but he was my rock throughout the ordeal. Richard decided on a day of reckoning and sat me down to hit me between the eyes with the reality of what was going on, and how far into debt we were going. Although he never gave me an ultimatum, he explained that walking the path we had gone down for the past three years was no longer an option. Over the next few days we talked more than we had done in months.

I didn't know what to do. I was prepared to lose a lot, almost everything, but not my marriage and my family. And yet I couldn't give up on John, having got this far. It was Richard who came up with the idea that we had to downsize; sell the house and start again. He knew what it meant to me to get John back, and gave me his blessing to continue. Our family had been through a lot, but John was family too, after all. Even if he didn't know the financial, physical and emotional cost of what I was doing, I was sure he would be grateful in the end that I had managed to get him out of the 'hellhole' he suffered in every day. For me, he did seem to be grateful when I visited him, really opening up and appreciating what I was doing, and this made it impossible for me to give up on him now, despite all the hardships it would mean for me and my family. I hated myself for putting the family through this, but I stressed to them that I'd do the same if it was one of them rotting away in a prison in Bangkok.

My husband's support was wonderful and gave me a new lease of life. I had to keep my campaign in check though, to be more realistic, and more understanding of my immediate family. I made an effort not to be on the phone or internet when Richard was home, and devoted more time to my children. Every day I counted my blessings for having the unconditional love of a man like Richard, and it really hammered home how lucky I was to have such support.

* * *

I kept my ear to the ground regarding the movements of the Australian Prime Minister and Foreign Minister, and anybody else I thought could influence either the ratification of the Treaty or a Pardon for John. Foreign Minister Alexander Downer was due on the ABC morning programme one day, so I immediately swung into action. I had to get to talk to him on air about the Treaty.

I raced the boys to school and returned home to grab my files, and every scrap of information I had compiled over the years. I wanted to be prepared to bombard Downer with cold, hard facts so he wouldn't have the opportunity to fob me off. I called the radio station and explained why I wanted to talk to Downer, and the producer immediately gave me the green light. I thought my heart was going to jump out of my mouth—I was still incredibly nervous about the media and talking to such important people—but after we exchanged pleasantries, my questions flowed as if I was reading from a well-rehearsed script.

The Foreign Minister was taken aback by my knowledge of the International Transfer Treaty, its history and all its ins and outs, and commended me on my research. He didn't know I had lived this for three years. He went on to say that the Treaty had his full support, was now in the hands of the state governments, and that he hoped for a positive outcome soon. I felt elated. The Foreign Minister of Australia had listened to me. I knew the faceless bureaucrats in Canberra would also now take my concerns on board to get this treaty up and running, or questions would be asked.

Talking to Downer was a great confidence boost. I had now spoken directly to the Prime Minister and the Foreign Minister about the campaign for John, and both had listened. What more could I ask for?

* * *

Not everything was going as well as planned though. While the Treaty negotiations seemed to be on track, my progress with John's Pardon application was going nowhere fast. Months had flown by, and there was still no sign of the application being ready. The stumbling block was getting it translated into Royal Thai. Having been let down twice before, and with it now in the hands of the Australian Embassy who said it was in a complete mess, I really didn't know what to do. I explained this to Trevor Lund in one of my letters to him, and he offered to help.

Having put our house on the market and downsizing, my financial troubles were no longer dire, so I felt it might be a good idea to make another trip to Bangkok to sort a few things out and hopefully speed things along. I made plans to head over in June, and got right onto the task of organising everything I would need to bring. I needed, for John's sake and my sanity, to get this Pardon sorted. It had been a mill stone round my neck for two years.

A week before I went over, I had the Embassy send it to Trevor in Klong Prem so that he could have time to look it over and give me his thoughts. Over the next week, Trevor and a Thai lawyer, who was also an inmate, transformed it into a fully translated masterpiece. It was mailed back to the Embassy staff who were, to say the least, very impressed. John Doran's King's Pardon Application was eventually submitted in July 2002, shortly after I left Bangkok.

It had taken two years of red tape and setbacks, and in the end took two inmates to rescue the application. This fact was, to me, yet another of those miracles and selfless acts I kept stumbling across.

Trevor had told me that his own Pardon application was ready to be submitted, but for some ludicrous reason the British government would not send a letter of support with his application. This was a great setback for him, but I could not help thinking, and hoping, he would find a way around this.

While all of this was going on, I made my sixth visit to Thailand. John had seemed so down in his last letter that I felt a visit was urgently needed to pick his spirits up. No longer allowed to cook his own food, and considering he was already dangerously under-weight, this spelt danger as far as his health was concerned. I felt I really needed to be there for him, to show him support, and to assure him I was still working towards getting him out of prison, and home. At this stage I was a dab hand at finding my way around and checked in to the by now very familiar Sofitel to prepare for a week of visits to the prison and the Embassy.

I got up early and got a taxi to Klong Prem, anxious to see John. Since I was last there, the visiting system had changed and there was now a new building for registering visitors. I managed the new system easily enough and got in to see John at 9.15am. It was very obvious from the start that he had had enough. He looked so thin and weak, and was really despondent. Being punished for so long for such a stupid crime had taken its toll on him. I wondered how much more he could take. The Thai system is so cruel and cold, without care for suffering, and seeing how it affected him, I think I began to fully understand it for the first time, and I didn't like it one bit.

I hoped giving him some positive news about the Treaty might pick him up a little, and tried to talk about his son Jason, but he remained very distant. I put this down to his being too scared to cope with any further disappointment and rejection, and it became harder and harder to find something to say. Everything just seemed to be going downhill. I couldn't even console him with the food parcel I had brought because the rules on food had changed too. Now, he wasn't allowed take the food back to his cell. All he was allowed to take was a packet of cough lozenges. *Not bad for someone who has tuberculosis*, I thought wryly.

I remember feeling so upset and angry that anybody could be treated this way; to be simply denied the right to proper food that should be theirs if they want it. The callousness of the guards made me want to scream at them in fury. I could only stand there in despair and watch as the visiting hour finished and the inmates lined up to go back to their cells, their food taken away from them. That image will always stay with me, forever burnt into my memory. John just looked into the distance, lost and emotionless. For him it was just another day in Klong Prem, but for me, it was a dramatic decline in standards. I was choked up with tears, and seeing the inmates wander off in a line, not looking back, was one of the saddest things I have ever seen. God knows how they managed to cope. I knew I would never be able to cope with such despair and hopelessness. The injustice of it made me angry and even more determined to change this awful situation. It was at this point that I decided I would have to meet the Australian Prime Minister in person.

I could see the classrooms where Trevor Lund taught English in the distance, which distracted me from having a cry right there and then. I felt he was watching over me to give me strength, and it worked. I pulled myself together and headed out to the front of the prison where I waited until 1pm so I could register to see Trevor. An English-speaking guard asked for my hotel room number, which I thought was cheeky, but I was willing to take it in good humour so that I might have less problems getting in and out. If the guards were friendly, I was more likely to get a contact visit when I asked for one. With a wag of my finger I told him I was old enough to be his mother, smiling all the time. Soon, and sure enough, I was given permission to enter and visit Trevor, giving my lover boy a wink on my way past.

Trevor looked well and was in great form; in total contrast to John. We chattered non-stop, pausing only to laugh. It seemed so strange that Trevor's regular dose of sanity was what comforted me and stopped me from losing it altogether. And he was the one locked up for years in one of the world's toughest prisons. His help with the Pardon application was also so important that I doubt we would have got anywhere if it wasn't for him. Our visit was over too soon and we said our goodbyes, hoping to see each other again the next day. We knew by now never to make any firm plans or to place too much hope on anything being definite. The prison's constantly shifting goal posts had taught us never to take anything for granted.

I returned to my hotel, desperately needing to shower and unwind, and as I sat trying to think of my next step, I received a phone call from Jim Pollard, a journalist with *The Nation*, who wanted to meet me the next day. I agreed, figuring that I could do with all the coverage I could get. Kraisorn at the Embassy phoned regarding John's Pardon application. It was good to hear from him and I still felt very grateful for all the help he gave me when Jason's family had come to Bangkok the last time. I told him to expect a masterful Pardon application from Trevor Lund, and he was delighted to hear about the progress being made. Promising to keep in touch and maybe meet up before I flew home, I said my goodbyes and headed out into the town. I needed to get out, and buy some food, so I headed down to the supermarket to get my mind off things.

However, seeing all the fruit and vegetables beautifully laid out had exactly the opposite effect. It really upset me for some reason, and I wanted to cry out, to grab someone and tell them that my brother was seriously malnourished and emaciated, only a few miles away, while all this food just lay around in aisle after aisle of elaborate displays. All I could think about was the image of John standing there in the prison yard, so thin and ill-looking, stripped bare of everything except his prison tunic and shorts. I walked out with my head bowed, tears streaming down my face as, once again, I was hit by the huge, immeasurable gulf between John and I. We were only a few miles apart, but there was a whole world between the outside world and the deplorable prison system.

I was relieved to get back to my hotel and even more so when I received a phone call from Richard and the boys. I was so happy to hear their voices, but I didn't mention my little drama, as I didn't want to worry them. Richard was excited, telling me he had just heard from Malcolm Penn of the state Department of Justice that the Transfer Treaty was scheduled to be ratified on 26 July 2002, just one month away. I couldn't believe it. I was speechless, over the moon, and very relieved.

Thank God the day ended on a high note. I could hardly wait to see John the next day, to tell him the good news about the Treaty, and about the developments in his Pardon application. The next morning couldn't come quick enough, but I knew that what I needed most was a good night's sleep, and to wake up the next morning rearing to go.

* * *

I was due to have a twenty minute non-contact visit with John on my second day, so I only needed to take my documentation and some money to deposit in his prison account.

While filling in the registration forms I noticed a very camp looking Thai guy gazing at me, but with a silly grin on his face. I gave him a brief, polite smile back, and that was all he needed. Before I knew it, he was at my side. He asked if I needed help, to which I replied 'No thank you' very quickly. It was plain to see that he was high as a kite. I could not believe him being so brazen within the walls of the Bangkok Hilton, knowing guys were doing never-ending prison sentences for possessing small amounts of narcotics.

He rambled on about visiting his cousin in prison and then casually asked me if I wanted to buy heroin or cocaine. I nearly had a heart attack, and got out of the registration area as fast as my feet would carry me. In all the times I'd been to the prison, I'd never experienced anything like it, and couldn't wait to tell John. He'd get a kick out of that story.

What a difference a day makes! John came through his side of the 'chook pen', clean-shaven and sporting a haircut—it was a fantastic sight to see. We chatted non-stop and I felt he was getting his spark back. Giving him the news about his Pardon application and the call Richard had received about the Treaty put a smile on his face, but he also had some good news for me; the trustee who had taken charge of John's bag of food had miraculously spirited the bag to his building, so the emotional torture I had put myself through the previous day was in vain.

The journalist Jim Pollard was keen to meet John, so I asked him if it was it ok to bring him to visit the next day. John acted like he hadn't a care in the world, and said, 'No worries.'

We said our goodbyes and I headed to the prison shop and money deposit area, where I needed to deposit money for John, Trevor and Mick the Australian guy, whose Mum had sent me money.

It was already turning into a busy day and I wasn't finished yet. I called Jim when I got back to the hotel and we arranged to meet at 8am the next morning to travel to Klong Prem. My beautiful room resembled a tip, so I started to sort out the pile of books, clothing and food I'd bought, not only for John, but for Sister Joan and the prison library.

I needed to relax, and decided that night that I would head down to the hotel's cabaret bar. Although I was alone, I'd long since given up hiding away in my room, and loved to listen to the Filipino band playing. They remembered me from my last trip, and it was not long before they were singing every Beatles song they knew, just for me. It gave me a much-needed break, and for an hour or two I got to relax and think of nothing but love, peace and Liverpool.

My home town and football club had played a big part in my campaign. Apart from John being a huge fan, other things started springing back into my mind. There were the football strips donated to Sister Joan's kids by Bill, as well as another AU$2,000 Bill donated in exchange for a signed football the club had sent me. It was worth a lot of money with so many international stars having signed it, and as a true Liverpool fan, Bill just couldn't resist buying it, especially when he knew where the money was going. Poignantly, I also remembered that one of the first things I had bought John when I first came to visit was a Liverpool jersey, and he said he was keeping it hidden away until the day he was released, so that he could walk out wearing it as a free man.

* * *

Meeting up with Jim the next morning was great because besides talking to John and Trevor in the prison, I'd been surrounded by strangers. John is not a great conversationalist but it was good to see that he and Jim got on well. I sat back and let them get acquainted. Jim told John he would come and see him again, and asked if he could send him anything. John asked for books; either *The Lord of the Rings* or a book called *The Magician*. He said he needed a bit of fantasy and escapism, and I wasn't surprised.

After that I was back to getting as much press coverage of the campaign as I could. Jim and I headed off into the city; he had an appointment with the *ABC* South-East Asian correspondent Peter Lloyd. We sat over coffee and discussed John's plight, and after I updated them on the Transfer Treaty, I did a brief recorded interview to be aired in Australia the next day.

Jim suggested we go for a drink at The Bunyip Bar, a place popular with ex-pat Australians and Embassy staff, possibly because it was actually within the grounds of the Embassy. I called Warren to see if he was free for a drink—wanting to keep him on-side.

I was feeling a bit on edge but Warren, Johnson and the other staff members made me welcome, with the Ambassador's secretary congratulating me on all the efforts I had put in for John and other inmates. It was good to see the other side of the people I tended to dub 'the faceless bureaucrats', and I felt that maybe it was good for them too, to see us, the families of inmates, as normal, everyday people, placed in a very emotionally demanding situation we never asked for.

The next morning, I woke up with a blazing headache, no doubt due to too many freely flowing Australian beers. But I felt a lot worse than any amount of beer could make me feel. I felt really low, as if I were spiralling into a deep depression. All the emotions of the past week had caught up with me, and I felt like I had hit rock bottom again. I kept the curtains closed, left the phone off the hook, and cried myself through the day, praying for this cloud to lift.

* * *

I was grateful that I had something to do on Sunday to take my mind off my own problems, having arranged to meet Sister Joan and to bring some more much-needed clothes and toys, donated by friends back in Perth, to the Klong Toey slums.

I arrived at the Human Development Foundation's Mercy Centre to be met by a very jovial and welcoming housemother. Children were appearing from everywhere, with smiling faces beaming up at me, fascinated at the sight of this blonde *farang* woman looking very out of place.

We unloaded the goods and entered the building, which was once home to hundreds of children. Sister Joan had not arrived but was on her way. The kids gathered around me, giggling and chatting to each other. They were all indescribably cute, but one child in particular caught my eye. It was difficult to tell if it was a boy or a girl, due to the fact that the child sported a shaved head. I asked the housemother, who spoke English, and it turned out she was a girl; her name was Kaitrin. She looked about four years old but I was astonished to hear she was seven. Her arms and legs were as thin as pipe cleaners, and old scars covered them. They had shaved her head after a bout of head lice, but she was as bright as a button and her smile lit up the room.

I was told that her parents were both serving lengthy jail sentences in Klong Prem, and that she would be cared for at the Mercy Centre until she was 18. It was yet another sad story coming from the unseen side of Bangkok, but I figured this poor little girl would be well looked after and would never want for love and support with Sister Joan watching over her.

All of the other kids had wandered off after the initial excitement had worn off, but Kaitrin sat next to me drawing, and before long she was sitting on my lap, babbling away in Thai. I was captivated. I reached into one of my bags and pulled out a lovely pink Barbie doll nightie and a couple of brightly coloured dresses. She was so excited, jabbering away and jumping up and down, before running off to put on all three garments at once.

It was moments like this that made me feel so privileged to meet these kids. I was a world away from my comfortable life in Australia, but it was the lesson I needed to take off the blinkers and see what really goes on in the world beyond your own doorstep.

I had worried and fretted over having to downsize my life because of the rising costs of my campaign, but I would never be in absolute poverty, completely dependant on the kindness and charity of others like this little girl, and I had the tremendous and unconditional support of my family behind me. To bring some happiness, however short-lived, to this girl and many like her was its own reward and I felt privileged to be able to do it.

Sister Joan arrived full of apologies for being late, but as I told her about my new found friend, she knew by my face that I was smitten. We loaded the bags and boxes into her van and set off to her home for a bite to eat.

I was hoping to tag along with Sister Joan for the rest of the day, to get to meet some of the other people she cared for. I was fascinated by her work. We took off to an area that looked to me like a shantytown, the likes of which I'd only seen on TV before.

The make-shift huts were built only feet away from a railway track. It was chaos. Walking fifty metres into the slum, we came across an old lady who was living in what I can only describe as a large box with a tarpaulin covering it.

Sister Joan had been visiting her for a while, and believed she had been destitute for a long time, with no family to care for her. When Sister Joan found her, the woman had badly broken her leg, but had no means of getting it tended to, or even looked at. It was horrific. On seeing Sister Joan, she smiled and tried to sit up to greet us. We immediately set out to a local street vendor and bought her some food; fried rice, eggs and a bottle of coke. That was her daily request.

It was plain to see Sister Joan was loved and respected in this Thai community. She works from dawn to dusk helping the poor, sick and needy, and I felt blessed to be able to witness this angel at work first-hand.

With Kaitrin still fresh on my mind, I asked Sister Joan if she could find out more information about the possibility of my sponsoring her education and welfare. She had made such an impression on me, and I could not walk away and forget her.

After a fascinating day in which I was appalled at the poverty and amazed at Sister Joan's work in equal measure, I was dropped into central Bangkok. It was early evening, so I had enough time to buy some replica Liverpool shirts for my sons to ease my guilt somewhat, before heading back to the hotel to prepare for another big day on Monday.

* * *

Prison visits were not permitted on weekends so I was really looking forward to seeing John for the first time in three days.

It was unusually quiet at the prison that Monday morning. I raced through the usually laborious visiting registration, and to my surprise, John was waiting in the 'chook pen' for me.

'What time d'ye call this then?' he joked. He was in great spirits, and again clean-shaven and bright eyed, I was relieved to see. He always seemed to get better with every visit, his sense of humour resurfacing, and a noticeable spring back in his step.

We talked non-stop about family and his beloved Liverpool FC, and I nagged him endlessly about working on his Pardon application. Trevor was in a different building to John but had managed to get a message to him regarding putting the finishing touches to it.

John promised me he'd get on to it as soon as possible. It was fantastic to see him motivated, and I was so glad I'd come to see him. John had been so depressed over the past few months, but now it was like he was refocused, and he could see a future outside the walls of Klong Prem.

He gave me his food order for the next day's visit; pizza was top of the list. I tried to focus completely on this visit, as the next day would be my last visit before going home. It was a contact visit, so I hoped and prayed we wouldn't have a repeat of the last week, when he had the food taken out of his hand.

I always dreaded the last day in Bangkok; saying goodbye never got easier. I always felt like a cloud was descending on me, but we had come so far on this journey and in my heart I knew we were so close to winning the fight to bring John home. His Pardon was ready to go and the Treaty was going to be signed. Both options for getting him out looked like they might work, and John had started to hope again.

I met Yvonne at the cafe next to the prison, run by the prison officers' wives, which was a good way of getting my mind off worrying about John. Yvonne always managed to cheer me up when I was getting down. She had become a haven for me in between visits. Having lunch and chatting with Yvonne was a Godsend that particular day. She knew me well enough to see I was finding it tough, but she had a knack of pulling me through.

She had been to see the Australian women inmates next to Klong Prem that morning, and was going through the shopping lists they had given her. She was a lifeline to them and she looked out for them like they were her own family, going far beyond her call of duty. I loved her for that.

After a while, it was time to head back to Klong Prem and see Trevor Lund for the last time. Greeting me with the familiar smile from ear to ear, Trevor asked if I wanted the good news or the bad news first.

I opted for the good, and he told me that John's Pardon would be ready to send to the Australian Embassy by the end of the day, complete and ready to be submitted to the King's office.

The two-year wait was finally over. If there had been a way to get through the mesh and two sets of bars, I would have hugged Trevor to death. This guy was one in a million, and I was blessed the day he unexpectedly came into my life.

Once I had calmed down it entered my head: What was the bad news? Trevor had been compiling his own Pardon application over the past few years, but the obstacle he had was getting the British government to support the application and back it up with a letter of support.

He had received a letter that day from the British Embassy stating that the British government's policy was to not support the applications. This was unlike the Australian government's policy, and to me, didn't make a whole lot of sense.

I was devastated for Trevor; he tried to put on a brave face, and said he would submit the application regardless. He demanded that this news was not to ruin my day. He said he would be firing off a barrage of letters to British M.Ps and he would not give up.

It was not the kind of ending to our visit I had expected, but I knew Trevor was mentally stronger than most of the inmates, and would be fine. We said our goodbyes and I raced off to do a final food shop for him.

I still had a lot of loose ends to tie up and hurried around the city trying to get everything done, saying my thank yous and goodbyes, before finally falling into bed. The next day would be the dreaded last day.

* * *

I did not feel like breakfast, being too busy making John some ham, cheese and mustard sandwiches. I packed plastic shopping bags full of food, and mentally said a prayer that he'd get them.

I had arranged to meet a photographer friend of Jim Pollard's called Steve Sandford outside the prison, to take some photos of me to use for publicity. It was something I hated doing, but I knew it was necessary.

Everything went as smoothly as could be expected at the prison. John was once again waiting for me, but this time we were able to hug and sit opposite each other. He wolfed down the sandwiches and pizza, in between smoking like a trooper, and I was glad to see him looking content for the first time in years. John had always been a computer nerd before he ended up in prison, so we talked about him studying to brush up on his computer skills. He also said he might be able to put his ability to speak Thai to good use and become a translator. All this positive thinking was amazing, I thought. I hoped to God John would not spend another Christmas in Thailand, but we could only wait and see.

The time I hated so much had come; time to say goodbye again. I know it was as hard for John as for me, but counting our blessings for the past week's achievements was the only way to get through it. Thankfully, he was able to take all the food back to his building, so that was a big win. I was kicking myself that I didn't bring more though. We had a last hug and I told him to write, and promised him I'd be back with the key soon. As soon as he was out of sight I broke down crying.

I made my way out of the prison, wondering why it actually got harder every time. I sat under a tree outside the prison gate, feeling totally drained, and wondered how I was going to make it to the women's prison in an hour or so to visit two Australian women called Deb and Jane. I had promised their mothers I would visit, and this was my last chance, so armed with some magazines and a letter from Deb's mum, I hoped I would be allowed in. I sent through a selection of fresh food from the prison shop in advance, just in case, but I was eventually let in.

When I arrived at the visiting area, I was shocked at what I saw. The conditions were far worse than those in the men's prison. It was horrendous, and I didn't even want to imagine how bad the rest of the place must have been. Talking through a hole in the mesh, you could just about see and hear them, even though they were only three metres away. Trying to see them through the layers of bars, mesh and bruised glass gave the impression of a battery hen farm. I could not believe that human beings could be treated this way, and the thought chilled me to the bone. For their sake, I tried to hide my disgust. The girls were over the moon to see me, and through it all, we managed to talk about messages to their families back home. They were desperate for an update regarding the Transfer Treaty, which they would qualify for once the law was passed. We even managed a few laughs as we discussed everything going on back home.

Still, having a three-way conversation like this was one of the hardest things I've ever experienced. This prison system seemed intent on inflicting punishment on the inmates on a daily basis. They allow visits, but why don't they allow these visits to be humane?

The visit passed too quickly and it was soon time to go. The rollercoaster ride of emotions was seriously affecting me, and again I was in tears leaving the prison.

The stress and strain of it all was becoming too much, and I had the worst headache I'd ever had in my life. I got back to the hotel and slept for a few hours, but I couldn't wait to get on that plane and get back home, into the arms of my husband and kids.

Despite the emotional toll, I knew the trip had been a great success. I had managed to get John's Pardon application sorted out and submitted, having already heard the Treaty would be ratified soon. I had also managed to bring a lot of media coverage to John's campaign, and those of others, while bringing some much needed donations to the poorest of the poor in the Bangkok slums. What had started as my own, wayward attempts to get my brother out of a foreign prison was rapidly expanding to become a mission offering hope and much-needed aid to those who needed it most; those with no support and nobody to turn to, and for that, I was immensely proud.

— CHAPTER NINE —

A week after arriving home from Bangkok, I had to get straight into the work of moving to a much smaller house, so I got bogged down with packing up and all the dramas that come with it, but I was confident the Treaty would be ratified as early as the start of July. I had great faith in whatever Malcolm Penn from the Justice Department said.

We had to be ruthless in deciding what we could move and what could be sold or dumped, as there was no way everything would fit into our smaller place, and that took up a lot of time. But I still managed to steal a moment or two throughout the day and night to check e-mails and make phone calls, not wanting to miss any updates on the Treaty and its ratification. As ever, I was soon to find out that there were complications and problems and that there would be delays. The optimism I had felt when I first came home dissolved and once more I was left feeling frustrated and angry. I was told by various agencies that it was the Victorian State government holding things up. All states and territories had to sign off any administration arrangements before the Federal Government could ratify the Transfer Treaty with the

Thai ambassador in Australia, and for some reason, Victoria were dragging their feet.

I spent a lot of time, effort and money calling interstate government departments, only to be fobbed off at every turn. Bringing Australian offenders back from overseas just wasn't a priority for the powers that be, so for them there was no rush.

July came and went, and I was extremely disappointed and frustrated that we were now told the Treaty would be signed some time in September. I was devastated; the never-ending 'carrot dangling' of the authorities was just getting to be too much. I wasn't sure how much more I could take. Why were they delaying this? What was the problem? To my knowledge, John was the only Australian prisoner in Thailand not associated with narcotics or paedophilia, so from the outset I assumed he would be one of the first prisoners to be repatriated. From what I knew of the Treaty details, John seemed to qualify easily. He had by now served five years, whereas under the proposed Treaty you had to have served four, and he had no outstanding charges. John qualified on all counts, unlike some other poor souls who had been given sentences of fifty years or life, and couldn't apply for another eight years.

I was never told outright that John would be a leading candidate for repatriation, but having dealt with other prisoners' families in Sydney it became clear that his case would be a lot more straightforward than others, being a petty crime, and much simpler on all fronts. Because of this, I just had to stay determined. Here was a real possibility to get John home.

I made an appointment to see the Federal Minister for Justice, Senator Chris Ellison, who happened to have his office in Perth. He was the minister whose signature would seal the deal with Thailand, and I had been no stranger to his office over the past few years.

I was met by his senior advisor, Brian Pontifax, who is a very friendly and respectful young guy. He had been extremely sympathetic to me, and we usually went to a nearby cafe for coffee, to give a more informal atmosphere to what could be a tedious and tiresome procedure.

Brian assured me that the minister was keen to sign the agreement and was well aware of the effort I had put in to bringing John home. I aired all my concerns to him, feeling like a broken record, repeating that we were dealing with human beings, and not just names and numbers, and after our meeting I felt a lot more confident of a positive outcome, sooner rather than later.

I tried to distract myself from endless worry by concentrating on our new house, which needed a lot of work. I was also making a weekly visit to Hakea Prison to see foreign prisoners, a routine started when I first visited Aksal and the other Indonesian boys. A Thai national called Boon asked me to contact his consul in Perth, regarding his case.

I had already been in regular contact with the honorary Thai consul to West Australia, Brigadier William Jamieson. We had never formally met, but he was sympathetic to John's cause. Brigadier Jamieson told me the Thai Ambassador to Australia was visiting Perth, and was due to retire soon. This might mean even further delays as his replacement got to grips with his position and familiarised himself with the most pressing diplomatic matters. I wasn't prepared to wait another year. He told me that they had actually discussed me the previous evening over dinner, and I was slightly taken aback and a little flattered to hear that my name was known in such high circles. Brigadier Jamieson passed on the details of the Ambassador's hotel, and deciding I had nothing to lose, I called him to see if he could shed any light on a date for the ratification of the Treaty. It may have been pushing it, but it was the only way I could think of to keep the whole process moving along.

The Ambassador turned out to be really helpful and polite. He promised me that on his return to Canberra, he would have his secretary contact me and inform me of the latest developments regarding the Treaty. I was overwhelmed by his response, and wished I had brought the Thai government into the equation a lot earlier. The only downside was that the Ambassador was retiring soon, so his interest would be short-lived.

True to his word, the next week I got an e-mail informing me that the Thai Embassy were contacting the Thai authorities in Bangkok on my behalf, and would update me soon. This was so encouraging, and I made it known to the Australian Federal Government that I was now talking to the Thais. I knew they didn't like me sticking my nose in that far, but I'd long given up pussy-footing around.

The weeks passed agonisingly slowly and there was still no set date for the signing. I was haunted by my promise to John that we would have him home for Christmas. I knew that even after the Treaty was signed a new set of obstacles would suddenly appear, so time was really important.

I felt I was playing a never-ending game of cat and mouse with the various people involved. On top of all the Australian departments, I now had the Thai government to liaise with. As promised, the Thai ambassador again e-mailed me on his return to Canberra and informed me he was following up the Treaty's progress with the Thai Attorney General in Bangkok. As usual, I was keeping tabs on the whereabouts of Foreign Minister Downer and our Justice Minister Ellison, because they both needed to be present if the Treaty were to be signed. I knew they were both in Canberra, so I crossed my fingers and waited for the call.

I had spent most of the week in court supporting the Indonesian boys, so my mind was always in two places at once, but I kept up my usual routine. On 26 September, the last day of the trial, I sat in anguish and watched these poor young men go through an awful ordeal, and await their sentencing. By the end of the day I was emotionally drained. Racing home from the court to meet the boys coming in from school, I made a beeline for the computer to check for new mails. Just in case. I was in a mad hurry to get the housework done and dinner on, but was instantly stopped in my tracks by the presence of one e-mail. What I read absolutely floored me.

It was from the Thai Ambassador to Australia, informing me he would be meeting the relevant Australian ministers that day, to ratify the Treaty. This, he said, would be his last act as outgoing Ambassador. He said he wanted to let me know because he knew I had put my heart and soul into it for the last three years.

I sat staring at the screen, reading the e-mail over and over again. I was in shock, but in the best possible way. I just couldn't believe what the e-mail was telling me:

'I want you to be the first to know that the ratification of the Thai-Australia Prisoner exchange treaty will be done this afternoon. I hope you will be able to bring back your brother at the earliest opportunity.'

I was eventually brought back to reality by the phone ringing. I raced to it, thinking it might be Mum, eager to tell her the news, but it was Sue Cox, a senior officer from DFAT, to tell me the news. I excitedly interrupted her, telling her I already knew, and who had told me. She had been trying to call me all day to let me know, but there was a certain amount of irony to think that after all these years of e-mails and phone calls to numerous Australian government departments, it was the Thais who gave me the news I'd waited three years to hear. I could just picture her at the other end, shaking her head in disbelief and saying to herself, 'Mrs Singh has done it again!'

As soon as I hung up the phone I burst into tears. I was so happy and so relieved that all the pent-up emotions just flowed out of me. When I had recovered slightly, I phoned Mum, Richard and anybody else I thought might be interested, and told them the good news.

That night Richard and I celebrated with a few bottles of champagne, but it really hadn't properly sunk in exactly what had been achieved. Good news had been thin on the ground over the past few years, but here we were, about to get a Treaty signed between Australia and Thailand that would allow prisoners to return home. It was an historic moment, and it was all down to my perseverance and refusal to give up.

Waking up the next morning a little hungover, I had to pinch myself. I turned on the radio and was met with even more fantastic news. Aksal and Ilam were found not guilty, and were free to go back to their families in Indonesia. It felt like all my Christmases had come at once. Riding the crest of a wave, it was now time to get John's application forms for a transfer together. We were well and truly on the last leg of the journey. Or so I thought.

Although I was elated at the news, I knew I'd have to keep up the pressure on the various government departments. I made a routine call to Kerin Lenard at the Attorney General's Department in Canberra and without hesitation she agreed to forward me the relevant documents John would need.

I had been informed that the Australian Embassy in Bangkok would visit John in the next few weeks but I was not prepared to wait, so I printed a copy and sent it to John myself. As a back up, I called up Jim Pollard in Bangkok and asked him to download the document and post it to John as soon as possible.

* * *

Things seemed to be looking up for the whole family. I had just started working again after a lengthy break and I was confident John was busy working away on his transfer application forms, with at most a couple of months of red tape to work through before he would be home, if not before Christmas then very soon afterwards. After a few weeks though, the long and winding road of red tape seemed endless, and I could feel myself slipping back into a state of anger and frustration. Other people with family in Bangkok prisons kept phoning me, hoping I could shed some light on who would be returning under the Treaty, and when, but I was as much in the dark as they were.

A few weeks after John received his forms, the Embassy visited the Australian inmates to brief them on the news. Most already knew.

I called a very respected Australian journalist, Victoria Laurie, who wrote for *The Australian*, a nationwide newspaper. Within hours she was at my house and we hammered out a story.

The next day the shit hit the fan. I was at work when the paper came out, and journalists from TV and radio were calling work and home. Long gone were the apprehension and nerves at whose toes I was stepping on. That day I did radio and TV interviews and local M.P. Graham Edwards went on TV pledging to go to Thailand and help us in any way he could.

Unfortunately, Christmas was looming and most of the government departments were having their Christmas break, so although going to the media had rattled some cages, the birds had flown the coop for a while.

Malcolm Penn was doing his usual good work, trying to move things along, but there always seemed to be another department to pass through or another meeting to take place.

Soon, it became painfully clear; John would not be home by Christmas. I was bloody naïve to think he would be. I dreaded having to write the letter to tell him the bad news. John handles bad news better than I do, maybe because he doesn't build his hopes up about anything. Unlike me, who expects the world, only to be let down with a thump.

It had been three months since the Treaty had been signed and the only explanation as to the delay was that the Thai Corrections Department only met every three months, and were not due to meet again until February 2003. I was incensed by this blame game, and wasn't prepared to just let my anger smoulder. I knew I would be heard loud and clear by going to the national press. One week before Christmas, I decided I had had enough. I called a journalist friend who wrote for a national newspaper.

The next day, the story was picked up by national TV and my phone was ringing off the hook. By bringing some media attention to the situation, I knew I was hurrying things along at both ends, and that everybody involved, be they in Canberra or Bangkok, would know my name, and know not to delay my campaign any further. Over the next few weeks, the wheels of diplomacy finally started to turn.

I made sure the story kept a high profile in the media, to ensure it never left the public's attention. In February 2003 I was contacted by Norm Aisbett, a journalist with *The West Australian* newspaper. Norm had visited John in Klong Prem a few years previously, and was keen to write a sympathetic story about his plight. Up until that time we had chosen not to release a picture of John to the media. My parents were dead against it, but Norm wouldn't get print approval without a picture to accompany his copy. As John was soon to be home, Norm was keen to get his story out into the public domain, so this time I gave him the photos and our blessing to print them.

Norm's feature on John had a profound effect on many who read the story—I think it really hammered home to people what John had suffered for the past six years. My parents were very happy with the article, and I once again breathed a sigh of relief that my ongoing media dealings had been positive. A few days after the paper had printed the article, Norm called me and said a handful of people had contacted the newspaper asking if they could write to John. This kind of reaching out to John hadn't happened before and I was so touched by the strangers' kindness. Norm provided the telephone numbers and I immediately made contact, passing on John's contact details and my thanks for their interest. I then wrote to John to let him know to expect parcels and letters from people he didn't know! I know he would have been bemused by all of this especially, as he was due to transfer home very soon.

As the weeks passed by, I received a few phone calls from a woman named Paula, from Ocean Reef. She was very enthusiastic and friendly, telling me that her husband (also named John) and she had sent books and letters to John in prison, and to her delight, she had received a letter in response. I was over the moon at the thought that John had ventured out of his shell enough to make contact with other people outside the family. It was comforting to think that after he would get out of prison in Australia, he might have some friends; given that he had not lived in Western Australian for many years, he had lost touch with his old circle. In our phone calls, Paula and I talked about meeting up for a coffee, but with children and work commitments on both sides, the meeting never happened, and while everything else was going on I almost forgot about her.

* * *

It was Saint Patrick's Day 2003, and while we needed no excuse for a tipple, Richard and I were settling down for an after dinner Guinness to mark the special day. As usual, our rare moment of family togetherness was interrupted by the ringing of the telephone, and with a groan and a sigh I got up to take the call. My irritation quickly dissolved on hearing the familiar voice of Warren MacIlwain, the Australian consul to Thailand. I had waited years for this call and its unexpected timing caught me off guard.

Warren had the news I had been seeking for six years; he had called to advise me that John's transfer from Klong Prem back to an Australian prison had been approved by the Bangkok Corrections Department. Finally soaring over the last hurdle, I was ecstatic. I was overwhelmed and couldn't hide my elation from Warren, whose ears must have rung for hours afterwards, with my ecstatic shouts of, 'Oh my God!' I called the kids down from upstairs and told them the news, before calling Mum and Dad. We were all so happy and relieved that this day had finally arrived. John, my little brother, was coming home! He would be the first ever Australian prisoner to be repatriated from Thailand. Yes, he would have to serve the rest of his sentence in an Australian jail, but he was getting out of that inhumane hellhole so far away from everyone he knew and loved. I couldn't believe it. We had done it! All the pain, tears and misery, not to mention the financial and emotional hardships my family had to put up with, suddenly seemed worthwhile.

Over the next week or so I liaised with the Embassy and the various government departments in Canberra and Perth. But once again, it was clear that this process was not going to be straightforward and trouble-free. Potential dates for John's return were discussed, and we learnt that he was required to return to Australia on a direct flight; something only possible on Thursdays. In addition, many Thai and Australian public holidays also fall during March and April and prisoners are not permitted to leave prison on these days. It was becoming increasingly frustrating to come up with a date that suited all parties.

Just as John was constantly losing hope of ever getting out alive, I was beginning to despair. So many promises had been made, and so many deadlines had been set, only to be missed. If it wasn't my brother suffering in a squalid, foreign jail, I may well have simply given up. I was ready to cave in because I was just too weary.

Weeks flew past and John's date of return was moved back from 10 April to 17 April to 24 April. I was at the end of my tether. Going to work each day was terribly stressful, as all I could think of was what news would be waiting for me when I returned home; would it be good or bad? Just when we thought that the date of 24 April was locked in, I came home from work to receive a call from Malcolm Penn at the Ministry of Justice. His tone was ominous, and I instantly knew that the news he had was not good. The Federal Attorney General's office had informed him that the Justice Minister, Chris Ellison, was going overseas and would be unable to sign the documents allowing John to return to Australia on 24 April, effectively setting back his return by another month. I was both outraged and filled with disbelief. Shaking with anger, I told Malcolm I was putting down the phone in order to call Senator Ellison's office straight away, with the intention of raising hell. I tried my best to pull myself together and calm down, and made the call, getting hold of Ellison's adviser, Brian Pontifax. As calmly as I was able, I explained what I'd been told and he asked that I leave it with him. Brian knew more than anyone what we had been going through. Getting John back seemed so close and yet so far away with these continuous, ridiculous setbacks.

Later that evening, Brian phoned to let me know that everything was back on track for the agreed date, and that the information given to Malcolm was nothing more than someone in Canberra passing the buck. Such a careless action betrayed the lack of compassion I kept coming up against. Some people who are in a position to drastically alter the lives of others just didn't seem to care, as far as I could see. If only they could realise that behind those names and numbers were real people, and they were playing games with those peoples' lives and emotions. John was wasting away in a Thai prison and with the stroke of a pen someone had deemed it fit for him to stay another month, for no reason. My dream was to see John walk out of Klong Prem prison in Bangkok, and finally out of prison here in Australia, and these mental images had kept me going through the bad times. Still, I was thanking God that the fight was nearly over, as I wasn't sure how much more I could take of the blitheness with which John's life was treated.

As usual, money was tight, and another trip to Thailand seemed out of the question. I felt I needed to be there though, to make absolutely sure they would release John when they said they would. I contemplated selling my jewellery to get me there, as after witnessing so much poverty and suffering in Bangkok, material things no longer had much hold over me. My good friend Julie offered to lend me the money, but I could not bring myself to accept her generosity. It dawned on me that there was another option open to me. I had maintained a good relationship with the journalists who had supported John's cause over the past few years and many had expressed an interest in coming to Bangkok to follow John's story; after all, history was being made. So, after some enquiries and a bit of persuasion, in return for the exclusive story, I was offered the airfare and accommodation. For days, I agonised about accepting the media offer. It was my only way of getting to Bangkok but apart from genuine offers of help which had no strings attached, I had never accepted freebies of any description during the previous six trips. It didn't sit well, ethically, to 'sell the story', and I hated to think about how some people might interpret this. After wrestling with my decision for some time, it was the level headed Richard who came to my rescue. He made the sensible point that the media would do some sort of story with or without my blessing, and if I did this deal as an exclusive with one media group, it was a readymade excuse not to deal with the others who had been hovering around. It would also put more pressure on the authorities to definitely see it through this time. The world would be watching.

There were still a lot of problems to consider though. My re-entry visa was about to expire and Easter was looming. However, my mind was made up. I set out to get my visa, paid for by my mum, did some last-minute shopping, and before I knew it, Nick Taylor, one of the journalists with whom I was to travel, was at my house working out an itinerary. It was hard to comprehend that the next day I would be beating the well worn track to Thailand again. But this time it would be different. This time, John would be with me on the flight home.

At the same time, I was playing a game of cat and mouse with the Department of Foreign Affairs. They were worried that I was going to turn John's release from Klong Prem into a media circus, and I was quizzed about my plans. I did not feel it was any of their business if I travelled to Thailand, or whether or not the trip was assisted by the media. At a time of extreme emotional upheaval, it was interference I did not need, and I was unduly stressed by their phone calls. They were lucky they did not call to my door. I would have gone ballistic.

The day of my flight to Thailand came around very quickly and before I knew it I was en route to the airport, picking up Nick on the way. We met Ian Cugley, the photo journalist, who would be travelling with us there. I'd met both men before and was relaxed in their company. As on my previous visits to Thailand, I was disturbed by a sight I had unfortunately become quite accustomed to. In a country infamous for its child sex trade, the omnipresence of pathetic, middle aged and sometimes very elderly men, openly preying on the desperation of teenage girls, was a telling indicator of the dreadful situation many young Thai children found themselves in. It always sickened me to see a pretty teenage Thai girl on the arm of a 60 year old Western letch, adorned with garish gem stone rings and a mismatched hairpiece, not to mention the Hawaiian shirt with the protruding belly. It was exploitation, and it made my blood boil.

Arriving in Bangkok, we made our way to the hotel. By now, I was accustomed to staying at the Sofitel, but this time we were in a different part of town, next to Soi Cowboy, one of Bangkok's many red-light districts. I was streetwise, so the location didn't bother me, and from the outside the hotel seemed pleasant enough. On entering my room, however, I was pretty underwhelmed. The curtains and carpets were stained, and reeked of years of cigarette smoke. The toilet was overflowing, and I wondered if I could sleep in the bed. I tried my best to hide my disappointment from the guys, remembering that without their help I would not be in Thailand at all. So I steeled myself, and decided to just get on with the task at hand. While I was unpacking, I received a phone call from Julie. We had tossed around the idea of her joining me for this trip, but the timing was wrong for her, being in the middle of her exam period. But she had changed her mind in order to offer me some much-needed support. As a student of criminal justice, I guess she was able to argue that this was a case study too interesting to miss. As well as that, she felt she just couldn't leave me to do this on my own.

I was overjoyed to hear she was flying in the next day and would be staying at our hotel. I felt such relief, as I knew this time I really needed some emotional support, and Julie was one of few people who truly understood the nightmare through which John and our family had lived this past six years.

We had arrived on a weekend, and were unable to get into the prison, so I spent the first two days resting, with the knowledge that there would be no time for any when Monday came around and I could see John. He did not know I was in Bangkok, but I doubted he would be surprised to see me—he knew me well enough. When the taxi collected us from the hotel on Monday morning, Ian asked the driver to take us to 'the monkey house', the Thai slang for prison. I was so excited when I finally saw John's face coming through the visiting area. Nick came in with me, and the first thing I asked John was whether or not he was okay with Nick being present. John wasn't bothered by a journalist being present, especially when I explained the newspaper had paid for my trip, but he wasn't prepared to share in my excitement. It was with disbelief that I learned he had not yet been given official notice that he was being transferred to Australia, and as a result, he hadn't kept his hopes high. As one who had endured an emotional rollercoaster and promises of amnesties over the past six years, he was playing it safe, protecting himself from the agony of yet more disappointment. I tried to assure him that it was going to happen, but he was having none of it. Before we knew it, the visit was over and we were saying our goodbyes until the next day.

Nick and I then met Ian, who was waiting in a nearby café, and we all headed back to the hotel. It was at that point that I called Warren at the Australian Embassy to let him know I was in Bangkok. I had not contacted him earlier, as I had a feeling he would not be thrilled about me being there, in case I interfered with plans he had made regarding John's transfer. I think he already felt I was being too intrusive and forceful, and no doubt the thought of me having the media in tow would send him into a spin. We had a brief chat, before he informed me I would not be permitted to attend the leaving ceremony to be held at nine o'clock on Thursday morning. He said he had no say in the matter. Because John was going to be the first Australian to be repatriated back to Australia from Thailand, the Corrections Department decided to hold a leaving ceremony. I hadn't been aware of any such formalities until the prison's Foreign Affairs Officer, Khun Thitiporn, started to update me on my daily visits leading up to John's release, but now I knew about it, there was no way I wasn't going to be there. I started planting seeds in the officer's mind that I desperately wanted to be there.

Out loud, I heard myself say, 'That's fine,' to Warren, but to myself, I thought, just bloody watch me! I respect authority, and I appreciate that for the most part, rules are in place for good reasons. But sometimes they're not, and if I had played by the rules over the past six years I would never have achieved anything in my fight for John's transfer. So I had developed a new motto: *Rules are meant to be bent or broken!* Warren asked me to keep in touch, and we said our polite goodbyes.

Later that day, Sister Joan, Yvonne, Julie and the journalists met in the lobby café for a drink. The photographer, Ian, had been to Thailand numerous times and had taken many brilliant pictures of Sister Joan working in Bangkok. It was actually his story about her three years earlier that inspired me to meet this amazing woman, so I owed him a lot. Without his story I would never have met Sister Joan, and without Sister Joan I would never have seen what suffering and poverty there was in Thailand. I felt buoyed by the knowledge that I was surrounded by so much support. We all had a great chat and a few cold beers, for at last we had something to celebrate. It still seemed surreal to me; it just didn't sink in that John would be boarding a plane back to Australia in three days, with me beside him! I had bent enough ears and trod on enough toes to make sure I was allowed to accompany him on the plane home, and I will be eternally grateful to all those people I probably drove mad over the years, in both Thailand and Australia.

I had also arranged to meet Dr John after visiting John because I'd requested all his x-rays and medical reports, to bring back to Australia and pass on to the prison hospital in Perth. One of the conditions of his transfer was that his T.B. was to be monitored, and any other health problems, such as his teeth taken care of.

I waited near gate two for Dr John; he sent a message to say he was delayed. One of the guards who had always been so kind to me sat down next to me, and started to talk. His English was not too good, but we managed a conversation about our families.

He then asked if I had an e-mail address, and went on to say his daughter was learning English, asking if I would write to her. I was flattered and more than happy to exchange information, but it caused a bit of a stir with the other guards lazily sitting round. They obviously got the wrong end of the stick, until they were scolded into silence.

Just then Dr John emerged through gate two; everyone jumped to their feet and greeted him with the respect he commanded. As a very short, slightly built man in his 50s, he always looked immaculate in his grey safari suit. We shook hands and he congratulated me on my efforts in bringing John home. From the Thai side of things, Dr John had witnessed first-hand the highs and lows I had endured over the past five years. He had been a great support and I will always be indebted to him for that.

He gave me a large package containing John's x-rays and reports, and I felt it was a moment of great meaning; a symbol of the fact that John was really coming home, and feeling the tears welling in my eyes, I shook his hand, thanked him, and headed back through the prison gate.

I headed off into peak hour traffic, which in Bangkok spells disaster. I was well and truly out of my comfort zone staying at the Tai Pan hotel, and after being stuck in traffic for over an hour I decided to get out and walk. I was convinced I was ten minutes away from my hotel on foot. I walked and walked for nearly one and a half hours. It was stinking hot, sickly humid and the polluted air from the bumper to bumper traffic was nauseating. The package containing John's medical reports had started to disintegrate from my sweaty palm clutch. I was lost.

I eventually crossed Sukhumvit Road and hailed a cab, and luckily, was back at the hotel within 15 minutes. It was now 6pm, I'd been out of the hotel since 8am, and I was totally exhausted. Nick and Ian had been wondering where I'd got to, so I let them know I was back and then crawled up to my room for a shower and a much needed rest.

I was woken by the telephone; I was still half-asleep but soon awake. It was reception informing me that if I wanted to bring someone back to my room later that evening there would be a charge of Baht 500. I could not believe my ears, but I politely declined the offer, which brought home to me why, in the past six trips to Bangkok, I had stayed at the Sofitel and not in the red-light part of town.

The next few days sped by, and another step towards cementing John's return came when I went shopping to buy him some clothes. He still had his special Liverpool football shirt we had bought him three years ago, hidden away in a bag for his big day, but still needed pants and shoes. It seemed my final day in Bangkok was going to be so different from my last six trips; there would be no tearful goodbyes, only beaming smiles and laughter.

Background music is the soundtrack of our lives, and often random coincidences can be spectacular. On Thursday morning at breakfast, the restaurant PA system was playing *Hope of Deliverance* by Paul McCartney, a favourite son of my native Liverpool. The sentiment of the chorus, 'Hope of deliverance from the darkness that surrounds us,' suited the moment perfectly, and ever since, this song has always reminded me of the day of John's transfer to Australia. As the music filtered through the restaurant, I looked up from my breakfast and quietly said, 'Thank you, God', acknowledging yet another one of those miracles that were repeatedly bestowed on me in Bangkok.

After the ceremony at 9am, John was due to be taken to the Immigration Detention Centre in central Bangkok, ahead of our 4pm flight home. On arriving at the prison at 8am, I could see Peter Lloyd from the ABC and other media waiting. This was the jolt I needed. The reality of John's impending transfer moved from the abstract to the immediate, causing me to burst out in torrents of tears of happiness, and making me shake like a leaf with emotion. As we made our way inside the prison, my lips trembling, I was still not sure if I would be allowed at the ceremony, but within a few minutes I was asked by a high ranking prison official if I would like to attend. Needless to say, I was overjoyed, and needed no further invitation. I pulled myself together, not wanting John to see me as a blubbering wreck, and in a flash I was up those stairs leading to the room where the ceremony would be held.

I was surprised to see a dozen or so officials dressed in their Sunday best, seated around a beautiful, carved teak table. It was a far cry from the third world conditions of the prison itself, only a hundred metres away. Warren and Kraisorn from the Embassy were waiting there, as well as the two Australian prison officers who had been sent over to Thailand to escort John on his return journey. I told Warren I was invited and he seemed genuinely happy for me. This was also a big moment for him, having to address the high-ranking personnel of the Corrections Department. He had to make a good impression for the benefit of future exchange prisoners languishing in Thai prisons. I asked Kraisorn if he would take some photos for me, as this was a moment I had waited six years to see, and being present to witness what was happening made every tear of frustration I had shed for John seem worth it.

It was an extraordinary feeling to be standing there with the governor of the Bangkok Hilton, and watching John enter the room, resplendent in his Liverpool shirt, wearing normal clothes for the first time in years, was simply mesmerising. John just looked bemused by all the fuss being made over him, and when he sat next to me it was all I could do to hold back from giving him a big hug. But that kind of emotional display was not the done thing in these formal circumstances. The officials said their piece, and Warren and the Governor shook hands. I was surprised and touched when my work in providing books and reading glasses was mentioned and I received a generous round of applause. As the ceremony wound down, we all applauded, before the media was invited to join us.

Peter Lloyd fired some questions at John while I stood behind him like he was a ventriloquist's dummy, feeding him one-word answers to repeat. We were giggling like a pair of kids, largely out of nervousness. John was then escorted out of prison to a paddy wagon, to make the half-hour journey to the Immigration Detention Centre. Seeing him take his first step beyond the prison door was a dream come true. We waved goodbye, and were quickly on our way in a taxi, following him all the way. I didn't want to let the police van out of my sight. I was feeling unusually relaxed though, stunned by the moment. We reached the detention centre to find John there, under lock and key in a sort of cage. This set me back a little; to see my brother locked up like an animal, and though I'd seen him behind bars and mesh, it still seemed unnecessarily inhumane to me to have him imprisoned like this. Did it have to be a cage? I sat on the floor outside his holding pen, and we tucked into hamburgers and soft drinks, and much to John's delight, we were able to smoke.

Oddly enough, there was a telephone in the cage, so I bought John a phone card so he could ring Mum and Dad, and my husband Richard and the boys back in Australia. Although it was the first phone call John had made in six years, he still remembered the phone numbers.

Yvonne arrived, and it all seemed so normal, the three of us having a chit-chat in such a surreal setting. Yvonne often visited prisoners in the detention centre, so she was undaunted by these inhumane surroundings.

Nick and Ian were waiting outside, as it was time to leave for the airport, and we wanted to arrive before John did, so that Ian could get some photos. Waiting at the airport was nerve racking, as I worried about last minute setbacks, but after 15 minutes a white van pulled up. The two Australian prison officers and Warren and Kraisorn escorted John to the check-in counter. At this moment, all the emotions I had stifled now rushed out into the open when I saw John outside the prison and the cage for the first time. I put my arms around him and sobbed like a child. The fact that he was handcuffed to a prison officer did not seem to matter to either of us. We walked towards the check-in desk when I realised armed police also shadowed our party. One of them gave me a smile and muttered something in Thai. While the officers checked in with John, I did my best to compose myself. Then Warren approached me saying, 'I know this is not exactly a good time but have you got Baht 500 (roughly AU$25) for John's departure tax?' After I recovered from the initial surprise, within seconds I handed the money to him. I couldn't believe I hadn't thought of the airport tax either.

We made our way to the departure lounge where the question arose of whether or not John would be handcuffed during the flight. It was a decision for the pilot, who agreed that as John's crime was so insignificant, he was not a threat to the passengers. I kept my distance from John and the officers, and tried to respect the fact they had a job to do. Once we boarded the plane it was fantastic that we were sitting in the same cabin, about ten rows apart. John had a window seat and the officer was sitting next to him. I will never forget seeing him eating his first meal on the plane. In addition to wolfing down his main meal, he also ate six bread rolls and three desserts, before settling down to watch the in-flight movie. Every now and again I would look back and see him, and remind myself that it was not a dream, it was a dream come true. We had made history. There was no legislation to allow a prisoner to return to Australia before this, but we had forced them to make it law, so that we could get John home.

It was approaching midnight when we flew into Perth airport. I took one final look back at John, and as the plane touched the runway, I clenched my fist and let out a loud, 'Yes!'

'Thank you God, thank you God,' I said to myself. We made it.

* * *

After we arrived back in Australia, John and I said our emotional goodbyes before he was whisked off to a private section of Immigration to be processed. As he was being led away by prison escort officers, we waved at each other, as casual as if we were waving to old friends on the street, and then he was gone, taken away to Casuarina Prison.

I was met by several really good friends at the airport, despite it being past 1am. Arriving home, I collapsed into bed, having well and truly burnt the candle at both ends. I needed to close my mind to everything, so I took the phone off the hook for a few hours and caught up on some much-needed sleep.

As soon as I was up again I was inundated with media questions, it being an historic occasion after all, and I had to call a halt to it after a while, being too mentally drained to keep answering them.

Later that day, John called from prison, and it was amazing to hear his voice and know he was only one hour away, and not in another country. He described with great pleasure how many sausages, rashers and eggs he'd had for breakfast, seeming very upbeat and taking everything in his stride. His biggest shock, he said, was sleeping in a bed with pillows for the first time in six years. He was still being kept in the hospital wing of the prison so they could monitor his health, but he had his own room and it wasn't long before, having really settled in, he was given a much-coveted job as hospital cleaner.

The television, radio and print media all ran their stories, so I presumed half of Perth would know, including Paula, the woman who had shown such an interest in John just before he returned, and her husband John.

When Mum and I visited John for the first time in an Australian prison soon after, he asked for Paula's phone number. Later that day, I called Paula to ask her permission to give John her number, and I learnt, to my surprise, that she did not know John was even back in Australia. She was keen to hear from him, and he called her soon after. This was to be the start of their friendship.

—CHAPTER TEN—

Throughout this journey I'd encountered so many forks in the road, but I felt it wasn't over just yet. All the time we were fighting to get John back to Australia, we had also provided support for his son Jason, but the main focus was still on John himself. I was for the most part concerned with getting him home so he could get on with his life and move on to greener pastures.

But when we finally achieved this aim, I couldn't help myself from thinking about Jason, living with extended family in the poor North-East Thailand, without a mother or father. Mere Luom had also died in the meantime, so he had lost another parent-figure. My family had given a lot of support, paying his family so that Jason could meet me and visit John in prison, and paying for his upkeep and education, but I just felt we had to do more.

John and I had spoken at length over the years about the possibility of bringing Jason to Australia, and John knew he had the support not only from Richard and I, but also Mum and Dad, my brothers and their families. We were brought up with a strong belief that 'family comes first,' instilled in us by our working-class Liverpool roots, of which we are so proud. So although Jason was living in another county, he was still family, and we wanted him to have all the opportunities our kids had.

As well as this, John had settled into Australian prison life unbelievably well, enjoying his job and putting on a few kilos a week, so I thought he was well on the road to recovery and would be able to handle having a child.

In September 2003, I was having lunch with Sister Joan Evans, who was back in Perth for some well-deserved rest and relaxation. We sat at a beachside café, catching up on all the news from home and Bangkok, and the conversation soon turned to Jason. I was still trying to keep in touch with Jason's carers, but it was difficult, and I was becoming more and more curious as to how we could bring him to Australia.

I've always valued Sister Joan's opinions, and when she explained that Jason would no doubt have a bleak future in North-East Thailand, and that he was at a good age to be able to adjust to a new environment, I needed no more encouragement. My mind was made up. I wanted to reunite Jason with his father; for good.

That night I spoke to my husband and mother and told them my plan. With a bit of persuasion I got them onside, and started to draw up some plans to go to Thailand and see about bringing Jason back with me.

This new campaign coincided with another venture I became a part of, and gave me two good reasons to return to Bangkok, which I fully intended to do. I was still deeply interested and involved in the goings on in Thailand, with the foreign prisoners in Bangkok jails and the desperately poor of the slums. As well as developing a good relationship with Sister Joan, I was still writing to Trevor Lund in Klong Prem, who was filling me in on everything that was happening inside the walls of the prison. I remember his letters over the course of the campaign. They shone like beacons of hope whenever I felt frustrated at government bureaucracy and doubted if I could go on. When the Treaty had been ratified but John's application was still pending, my morning walk to the mailbox was like opening Pandora's box. One thing that always lifted my spirits was a letter from Trevor. Although he was thousands of miles away, he seemed to understand my feelings and always managed to pull me into line.

As soon as I had returned from Thailand with John, I received a letter from Trevor asking about the ins and outs of the case and wishing John luck for the future. It was so thoughtful of him. But Trevor would amaze me further still.

In one of my letters to him the previous year, I had joked about him running the Bangkok marathon, but inside the prison. Trevor did run every day to keep fit, but I meant it as a joke. However, for Trevor, nothing is impossible; what started out as a joke by me turned into a reality for Trevor, and I was soon recruited for an amazing charity campaign.

Trevor outlined a plan in a lengthy letter, which would involve his contacts in the UK, Yvonne in Bangkok and me in West Australia, and after a few phone calls, our plan started to take shape. Trevor was going to run a marathon inside the prison grounds, and we would try to get as many people from all walks of life to sponsor him. He came up with the idea that all the money raised would go to Sister Joan's mission. It was a wonderful idea and I relished the chance to find more donations for such a good cause. If it could help raise Trevor's profile to aid in his application for a Pardon, all the better.

Trevor wrote to the Thai Corrections Department for permission, as this kind of event had never been thought of before. He also wrote to Sister Joan, asking her if she would be willing to accept the money raised. Needless to say, she was delighted. After that, it was just a matter of raising some money and taking it from there.

I thought back to the success I had selling the Liverpool shirt for Sister Joan's charity, so I started to make enquiries into that, with a view towards maybe holding an auction in Bangkok. My cousin Carl had visited Trevor when he was in Bangkok and had been very taken with him, and fortunately, he had won a trip to Liverpool FC's football academy. So when he heard about Trevor's plans, he took his chance and at Anfield he asked Michael Owen to sign a Liverpool shirt for the charity. Owen was happy to oblige and the shirt was sent straight to Yvonne in Bangkok. It was a great start. With a lot of intensive begging and pleading, we also managed to get a signed shirt from the late, great George Best, so we had some really good items we hoped would raise a lot of money.

I'd read an article about an Irish businessman supporting prisoners in Thai jails, so I contacted him and asked if he could help us promote the event in one of his

Irish pubs in Bangkok. He was very enthusiastic and also offered me accommodation for my stay. I was blown away by his generosity. In my previous trips to Bangkok I'd never had such an offer, and from a complete stranger!

My flight was booked the next day, work was notified and my plans were underway. My plan was to spend the first five days in Bangkok for the marathon and then head up north to Somdet to see Jason and his carers.

Once again I was on my way, cases overloaded with gifts for Jason, clothing for Sister Joan, and not forgetting the precious football shirt signed by the famous George Best for our auction in Bangkok.

This trip felt so different to the past seven; John was not there, so there would be no heartbreak and stress at saying goodbye and leaving him behind. Instead, I was filled with excitement; it felt like a real adventure.

On arriving at the hotel I was amazed at how luxurious it was, but I had little time to enjoy my surroundings as the next few days were spent racing round with Yvonne, having tee shirts printed, gathering sponsors, and of course, seeing Trevor, whose training was going well.

The Foreign Affairs officers at Klong Prem were fantastic, letting me see Trevor every day. When Saturday evening arrived, Yvonne and I arrived at the Irish pub looking like a pair of nutters in our green and white 'Trevor Lund, Klong Prem' T-shirts. Five years before, I could never in my wildest dreams have pictured myself doing this, but I dived right in and gave it my all, drumming up support and cash for Trevor.

That night was one to remember; it was the Rugby World Cup final between Australia and England, so the atmosphere was electric and the beer flowed like a river, and in the end, nobody was in any doubt as to what we were doing and why. At the same time, the whole campaign was chopping and changing and new angles and aspects were being brought in at every hand's turn so changes were made, then forgotten about, then made again. The chief of the prison decided it might be a good idea for other inmates to take part, so the plans changed again.

At one stage in the evening, I got a call from Steve Sandford, the freelance photojournalist. He asked if I wanted to act as his assistant to get inside Klong Prem and witness the marathon myself. He didn't have to ask me twice.

We met at 6am, and taxied our way to the prison. Trevor must have got quite a shock when he saw me walk through the prison gates. He had no idea I would find a way to get access, but by this stage, he knew that small miracles tended to happen whenever they were most needed.

The marathon had started and Trevor and the guys were running their hearts out. The Director of Klong Prem was walking around, adorned in a tracksuit, trying his best to look the part as we all looked on. After a while he joined me and we ate breakfast together. He spoke no English but had one of his officers ask me if I would be willing to help organize the next year's marathon.

It was so surreal, going back to the place where my brother had been incarcerated and forced to suffer terrible conditions for six years. Here I was, inside the Bangkok Hilton, mixing with inmates and officers, having breakfast with the Commander, while Trevor and 15 other inmates ran the marathon outside the window. I kept thinking to myself: *Pinch me, this can't be real.* But it was.

Trevor would pass by the window roughly every five minutes on each lap of the grounds, and he looked to be doing well. With one lap to go, the finishing line was set up and I was ushered in to hold the blue tape for the winner to cross. I could see Trevor in the distance, closely followed by an inmate from Laos. The final stages were amazing; a magic moment I will always feel privileged for having witnessed. These men, all of whom had been in prison for many years, managed to achieve their goal with dignity and courage.

The whole thing seemed to be a great success. It was a great morale boost for the runners and a great PR triumph for the Thai Corrections Department. Trevor won the marathon, got international media coverage, and most importantly netted Sister Joan Baht 120,000, just shy of AU$5,000.

I was so proud of Trevor for what he had done. Without him, this day would never have come about, and with his ideas and determination he had changed the lives of so many, not only within Klong Prem but in the poor slums of Bangkok where poverty is itself a prison few can escape.

* * *

With the marathon over it was time to concentrate on the main reason for my trip. On so many of the other visits to Thailand, I'd wanted to go to the village where Jason lived, but my focus was on John and devoting my time to visiting him in Klong Prem. Now, at last, I could set out to see this little guy whose pictures had adorned many walls in my home for the past four years.

With a stroke of luck, I'd met an Irishman called Norman and his beautiful Thai partner Nat. Norman had offered to help me organise travelling to Kalasin in North-East Thailand, and Nat travelled with me to translate. My Thai was non-existent, so this offer was too good to be true. We decided to travel by train overnight to Khon Khan and then catch the bus to Somdet. We arrived at the station, me the only Westerner, surrounded by a mixture of Thai society. Everybody had a smile for me, which I found wonderful. Whether they were being friendly, or just found my oversized presence amusing, I'll never know.

Nat was a gem, tending to my every need, and it was hard to believe I had only met her days before. I felt she would be part of my life forever. After a restless night on the train, around 6am we inched our way into Khon Khan. I was worn out but still excited at having finally made it.

I felt the nerves setting in as we neared Jason's village. I was surprised to see that it was far from being a rural outpost, and had a lot of shops selling much the same stuff as you would find in Bangkok. Nat called the mobile number we had, and the family said they'd meet us in 15 minutes. They pulled up in a minivan taxi, which they had hired for the day, and I instantly recognised Pashwai, Boon Luom's son in law. I was a bit taken aback by the fact he was drinking a beer, at this hour of the morning. There was a strange atmosphere. I was greeted warmly, but sensed I was being weighed up for what I was worth. I tried to tap into Nat's body language because I certainly did not know what was being said. Jason then emerged from the van, looking tiny for his six years, but as cute as a button.

I wanted to give him a big hug but held back so as not to frighten him, but when he gave me a big smile I felt more at ease. Within minutes we were walking towards a street market, so I asked Nat to ask what the family would like to eat for breakfast. Before I knew it, we were standing at a bike store. I think at this stage Nat and I knew what was expected of the big blonde *farang* woman. Money.

I had sent money, as had Mum, on two previous occasions, so that they could buy Jason a bike, but he had obviously never got it. Jason's face lit up when we got to the bike market and he saw a small red one that would suit him perfectly. Pashwai interrupted him though, and coerced him into choosing a more expensive one. I kept calm, but I could see Nat was becoming increasingly frustrated by their actions. She later told me she was embarrassed by their trying to take advantage of me.

So Jason got his bike, and then we went for breakfast. Pashwai, the young guy, had a Singha beer in his hand throughout the morning, obviously not stopping at one. I didn't like what I was seeing, and I was grateful that I had decided to make this trip, to see exactly what Jason's conditions were like. I knew they were poor, but I still felt like they were only interested in me for one reason, unconcerned with Jason's welfare or what was in his best interests. I was distraught, but tried to keep a smile on my face because I wanted everything to go well and for us to get along. Causing any upset at this early stage would be devastating. We went to a food stall and I told the family to load up several bags to bring to their home. They didn't have to be asked twice.

We checked into the local hotel, which was infested with cockroaches, and I was not feeling too happy, to say the least. I realised the game was on, and I needed to sit down with Nat and plan how to deal with these people.

We arranged to meet outside the hotel and travel to the village where Boon Luom, the older man who had supposedly been Jason's primary carer, lived. We pulled up outside an old house on stilts and I could see that it was surrounded by what I would call wasteland. There were certainly no homely features.

Boon Luom greeted me with a handshake and I gave him a hug, as he seemed a nice man the last time we had met. I had come here with an open mind and a warm heart, so I wanted everyone to be happy.

Nat and I started to open up the many bags we had brought along, giving out the clothing, toys and a variety of food we had picked up in town. Neighbours and friends started to flock; and they were certainly not shy, helping themselves to the food bought for the hosts. The strange thing was that no one seemed to mind.

I felt reasonably relaxed but couldn't shake the feeling I was under the microscope, being assessed not for who I was, but for what I might offer. Everywhere I looked I was met with smiling faces, especially from Jason's carers, but again I got the impression that behind the smiles all they wanted me for was money, money, money, and I felt they were using Jason as their cash cow. I felt this was almost understandable due to their terrible poverty, but not when it put Jason's well-being after their monetary interests. He had to come first.

We all went to the local river, where Pashwai and Boon Luom were sitting down and knocking back whiskey, and it was still only 11am! Nat and I could feel their mood changing as the alcohol took effect and alarm bells just started ringing in my head. I played with Jason, who seemed fascinated by the water. He immersed himself up to his shoulders, screaming and laughing with delight, and I knew then that this little boy would be worth the effort to bring to Australia. Although these people did care for him, it was plain to see Jason did not have a mother or father figure, which I found desperately sad.

Nat and I had a good chat later that day about what we had seen, but she also filled me in on what I had missed. Boon Luom had complained to her that I, the *farang*, had not sent any money for Jason's upkeep, which was completely untrue. Two months earlier, I had sent

AU$500 to his daughter Saisuda's bank account. Luckily, I had all the bank details with me so later that day we set out to the bank to find out what was going on. Much to my surprise, the bank manager was very helpful.

He printed out a copy of the bank account, showing she had indeed received the money, but had spent almost all of it. This fuelled our suspicions that a lot of underhand games were being played here, but I didn't want to make trouble while still in Somdet, so we agreed to tackle the problem at a later date.

We headed back to our hotel, arranging to meet up with the family again the next day. I was worried they may have been disappointed in me and wouldn't turn up with Jason, but Nat figured my fears were groundless. The way she saw it, they were not yet finished with me and would be thinking of more ways that I could benefit them financially. Regrettably, she was right.

When we met the next day the family immediately wanted to go on another shopping spree, funded by me of course. Jason wasn't there, much to my disappointment, having miraculously started school since my last updates. I really wanted to see him, as Nat and I had to return to Bangkok later that day.

I wanted to see where Jason slept, and what kind of conditions he lived in, so I persuaded the family to let me come back to their house. I hoped to God he didn't sleep anywhere near Boon Luom, as his fondness for Thai whisky early in the morning didn't fill me with confidence. Nat tried to find out but was met with a lot of contradictory answers, so we remained none the wiser.

This just made me more determined to get Jason out of this situation.

As we said our goodbyes and made a few arrangements to keep in touch with the family through Nat, I silently vowed to make sure Jason would enjoy a much better life in Australia with John and my own family. But I was surprised when Boon Luom's daughter, the one with the busy bank account, asked if she could accompany us to Bangkok, where she would find Jason a better school. I agreed without hesitation. If Jason was in Bangkok, Norman and Nat could at least keep an eye on him and keep me informed. I had come to Thailand this time with the idea that John needed a connection with his son re-established, but on leaving, that idea had changed. I was now determined to make that connection a permanent fixture, with Jason living with us. It was the only way I knew I could guarantee his welfare.

— CHAPTER ELEVEN—

I was so looking forward to stepping over the welcoming mat at my own front door. Even though it was 1am, I knew the boys would be awake, or at least half asleep on the couch, waiting to open up my suitcases in search of presents, and to ask endless questions. I had so many photos to show them, and stories to tell, that we fought off sleep until 5am.

Trying to get back into a routine proved as difficult as ever, but once I was back at work things settled down. John was calling daily from prison and we were going over the many good and bad things I had encountered in Thailand. We also spoke in-depth about the red tape we needed to tackle to get Jason to Australia. John and I shared our thoughts and agreed that Jason should live with John in our home. Richard and I were already mulling over the thoughts of moving to a bigger house as soon as John was free.

It was good for John to have something positive to focus on, and he seemed happy with the progress I had made. He said he was looking forward to the prospect of seeing Jason in the new year.

Norman and Nat, my guardian angels in Bangkok, were calling almost daily with updates, as they were keeping in touch with Jason's carers by telephone. A few weeks passed and Norman informed me that Jason had still not been enrolled in school, so we started to wonder what was going on. After all, I had given them money for his education. Another matter of concern was that every time Nat spoke to Jason's carers, it turned out he was out with Saisuda, the daughter's brother, and her partner, who worked very late every night.

About this time, Nat and Norman had decided to take a break at a seaside resort near Pattaya, one-hour south of Bangkok. Norman called me and suggested they should offer to take Jason for the weekend. I was happy about this but thought there was no way the carers would agree. But late that evening I got a call from Norman saying Jason was with them and was happy to go on holiday with him and Nat.

I could not believe this. My first instincts were to jump on a plane and bring Jason to Australia. After I calmed down, Norman asked me if they should keep Jason with them until I could get back to Bangkok, and without hesitation I said yes. At the end of the day, Jason was not being looked after, and we needed to know he was in safe hands. I trusted Nat and Norman completely.

I called Mum and Dad and explained the situation; they were overwhelmed by the thought that we could at last lay down the plans to bring John's son, their youngest grandson, to Australia.

Mum had only seen Jason when he was three and Dad had to make do with photographs.

When John rang the next day I couldn't wait to tell him the news. He was very surprised, just as I had been the previous day. I'd been thinking on my feet and already had the documentation that the Embassy had given me on request, so I posted everything to John and we swiftly got the ball rolling.

That weekend, I went on my weekly visit to see John in prison. I explained the red tape we had to get through to bring Jason to Australia and spoke in-depth about the support our family would give. Richard and I, and Mum and Dad would take good care of Jason.

It was plain to see John had a long, hard road ahead, getting his life back on track, and he would need a lot of support. It was great to see that he seemed happy and excited at the prospect of getting to know his son, a dream he had talked about many times from behind the bars at Klong Prem. I wanted more than anything to help fulfil that dream for him.

When Nat and Norman arrived back in Bangkok after their break at Pattaya, it became clear to Jason's carers that he was not coming back to them. They harassed Nat and Norman over the telephone, so we thought it best that they move to a hotel for a week or so. It was a very stressful time for them, and Norman's health was not the best. I needed to get back to Bangkok and relieve them of the huge responsibility they had taken on.

Once again though, I had to struggle with my conscience. Christmas was just around the corner and work was mad busy. Even worse was the fact that I felt so guilty abandoning my kids over the Christmas holidays, and once again found myself swearing I would make it up to them. Mum and Dad came to the rescue financially, and my flight was booked. I can still remember the shiver of excitement I felt when I looked at my tickets, with a single child's ticket kept in reserve beside it.

Although we still had a lot of hurdles to get over, nothing was going to stop me bringing Jason to Australia; we had come too far to have any doubts. I boarded the overnight flight to Bangkok, unable to comprehend it was Boxing Day and I was leaving my family yet again. I hoped and prayed more than ever for guidance, and somehow knew I was in safe hands. Norman, Nat and Jason were to meet me at the airport, so I could not get there quick enough.

I hurriedly collected my bags and raced to the meeting point we had arranged. I could see Nat's beautiful, smiling face, Norman beside her, and sitting on the rail was the cutest little boy, with his trendy, spiked fringe, giving me the biggest smile.

My heart melted. We had a three-way hug and kiss, and my thoughts were filled with questions as to how I could ever repay Nat and Norman for what they had done. We quickly made our way to the taxi stand and headed to my hotel. It was plain to see that Jason had bonded strongly with Nat. In their two weeks together, it was clear she had grown to love him.

Norman was going over all the dramas they had put up with over the past weeks, and I could see they needed time alone to rest and get their own lives back on track. After an hour or so they headed home.

Jason was upset when Nat left the room, but with some gentle persuasion and bribery we were fine. Nat had told him I would be taking him shopping for Spiderman and Batman toys, and that soon did the trick.

It was hard to comprehend that I was sitting in a hotel room with this little boy, who only a few years earlier, we didn't even known about, never mind tried to meet. We had fun and games getting around the language barrier, but one way or another we broke down the communication walls, sometimes in the funniest of ways. After a while, I started to feel a bit like Marcel Marceau, the famous mime artist.

Norman called the next day to see how we were doing. I was feeling very sorry for Nat, because she had formed such a strong bond with Jason, and I'm sure by now was feeling at a loss.

Norman and I thought it best that Nat did not visit Jason over the next few days, because it would give me a chance to get to know him and to gain his trust. It was so sad to think that this special little man had been passed from pillar to post so much in his short little life. Through no fault of her own, his birth mother had left him with extended family so she could work in Bangkok to support him and her three other children from a previous marriage. She had no choice; she needed to work in the city to make enough money to feed them. Then when she had moved to America, he just didn't settle at all and was brought back to Thailand to stay with a female relative.

After the lady who cared for him in his mother's absence had died two years before, he was then placed in the care of another lady and her father from the same village, before ending up with Boon Luom, Saisuda and Pashwai. Jason had only met his father once in this time, when he was three years old, so had little or no recollection of him. This sad story made me more determined for Jason to have a loving family now, and there was a big one waiting in Australia with open arms.

Over the next few days Jason settled down and we went on daily shopping trips to the markets of Bangkok. We were always met with a warm greeting from the stall holders, who would assume I was his natural mother and his father was Thai. Jason's strange form of Thai with a Laos dialect seemed curious to a lot of people, so while they found it a little funny, they also found it very endearing.

He was not backward in coming forward, letting me know which Spiderman or Power Ranger toy he wanted, and soon the hotel room resembled a toy shop. I was trying not to spoil him, but on the other hand I wanted to give him the things he'd never had before. Another daily routine was having lunch or dinner at K.F.C. Although he had lived all his life in a rural village in North-East Thailand, western influences had clearly reached him.

Amongst the fun and games, there were some serious issues to consider. Time was moving on and I only had three working days to arrange Jason's Australian citizenship and passport. I had liaised with the Immigration Department and Warren MacIlwain at the

Australian Embassy while I was in Australia, so I had a fair idea of what was needed.

John had signed all the documentation, and Jason's mother in America had signed the documents at the Australian Embassy in L.A. She too had been angered at the conditions we had found Jason to be living in. I arranged to go to the Embassy, and although it was a very detailed and nerve racking process, the staff gave their full attention to the situation, pulling out all the stops, including going into work on days off, to ensure we would both be boarding the plane on Friday.

I thought it would be nice to go see Trevor at Klong Prem. He had no idea I was even in Bangkok, so when I came into the visiting area with Jason he was very surprised to see me. As soon as he did, a wide grin spread across his face and he shouted through the bars and mesh of the 'chook pen', 'Hello Mum!' I gave him the rundown of why I was back, as I had only left four weeks earlier, and caught up on all the post-marathon stories. I only hoped the coverage the event received would in some way help him to get that Pardon he had been waiting so long to receive.

* * *

Tuesday, 30 December was my birthday, and having Jason with me was one of the best birthday presents I could ever wish for. We did our daily trek to the Embassy, and within a few hours I was given Jason's Australian citizenship certificate. This was a moment I will never forget.

I had plans to go to dinner and catch up with friends but Jason and I were totally worn out, so we settled for some take away food and, looking out the hotel window over the Bangkok night sky, I wished Richard and the boys were there to enjoy the moment. I missed them so much, and was counting the days to get back home.

Friday arrived and I had to be at the Embassy for 9am. We were close—all that was needed was a fax to be sent through from Immigration in Australia, and a passport to be issued. The morning dragged on and Jason was becoming sick and tired of all the waiting, and as we were flying out at 4.50 p.m. I was starting to panic. Of all things to set us back, the machine used for issuing the passports was playing up. Talk about a last minute hitch! What's my life without a drama, I thought.

At midday all was sorted, so I said my goodbyes and a big 'thank you' to the Embassy staff Warren, Kraisorn and Johnson, and headed back to the hotel to collect our luggage. I just wanted to get on that plane and breathe a deep sigh of relief, and Jason was so excited to be heading to the airport.

All I could get from him was '*Jimpany, Jimpany*,' which in Thai meant aeroplane, as we arrived at the airport. It was a great distraction because he had become unsettled over the past few days. I think he'd had enough of hotel rooms and wanted to be on his way to 'Ausdadalia', as he would say every five minutes. Finally, the time had arrived; even though the ink was still wet on his passport.

I knew I would face scrutiny at customs. A foreigner leaving with a Thai child always attracted attention, even though Jason was now, for the past four days, an Australian citizen, and an Australian passport holder for less than half a day.

Thank God Warren at the Embassy had suggested I have a written document in Thai from them explaining the situation. That did the trick and after five minutes we were on our way to the departure lounge. Jason was so excited taking off; he wanted to see out the window and he ranted in Thai for the next half hour or so. God only knows what he was saying but the main thing was that he was happy. He ate his meal, and then a kind lady sitting behind us offered him her Gameboy. For the next hour I didn't get a peep out of him.

* * *

Yet another miracle had come true. As I relaxed on the flight, I looked back over the past six years and couldn't believe that so many good things could possibly have come out of my brother being in prison in Bangkok.

As I recalled all the small miracles I had experienced in Thailand, one thing struck me; I could never have achieved all of these things; John's release, the Transfer Treaty, the donations to Sister Joan, my eyes being opened to the conditions of the poor of Bangkok; the marathon at Klong Prem, without the support of my family, and God for answering so many of my prayers.

Throughout this six year journey I had lost touch with so many people because I was so focused on my goals, and nearly lost my husband and kids, but sometimes you have to make sacrifices to gain, and I think looking back, I well and truly did that without many regrets. And I would do the same again.

* * *

Touching down in Perth, Jason was sound asleep and I was panicking at the thought of waking him up, because he always hated that, yelling and screaming at the interruption to his nap. On cue he kicked off, and because I was overloaded with hand luggage, we were the last to leave the plane. I struggled along desperately until a lady from Thai Airways approached with a wheelchair not in use. It was quickly loaded up with bags, and Jason sat on top of the luggage like the king of the castle.

We breezed our way through customs, and within minutes came into the main concourse, where Richard stood with his arms folded across his chest. His first words to me were, 'He's a little flea!' He was just taken aback by how tiny Jason was for a six year old.

At home the boys were waiting for us. I'm not sure what was going through their minds, but one thing was for sure; things would never be the same in the Singh household. We weren't sure what would happen and we just didn't know what to do. I mean, what do you do when you have a child who can't speak a word of English, and he's just standing there scowling? There is simply no blueprint for bringing a six year old boy from an impoverished village in North-East Thailand to beautiful, sunny Australia. We just had to take it one step at a time. Luckily, Jason instantly took to Michael, one of my nine-year-old twins, for what reason I'm not sure, and because it was school holidays, the boys had plenty of time to get to know each other. Our days were spent at the local park and swimming pool, getting Jason accustomed to our family, and he seemed to be enjoying himself immensely, always smiling from ear to ear. Even without any English, he was still somehow able to get across his wants and needs in no uncertain terms. He is a very strong-willed and determined little boy, and it was plain to see it had been a 'survival of the fittest' upbringing in his village. He outwitted the other boys so well it was almost a fine art, and Richard and I quietly thought this was hilarious.

We had tears and tantrums, as well as the smiles and laughter that make it all worthwhile, so it was pretty much how our family was before Jason arrived. We just tended to multiply the above ten fold, and thank God we had been blessed with the chance of bringing up this special little boy.

Nat and Norman were still in regular phone contact and Nat would often say a few reassuring words in Thai to Jason, which would settle him down and make him feel more secure. She was one of the few people who had won his confidence over the few months since he had left his village.

* * *

As far as John was concerned though, I could not in my wildest dreams envisage what was about to unfold. We had a surreal discussion which revealed where his heart was; I'd just been to the end of the earth and back, successfully returning to Australia in one piece with his son, but his mind was elsewhere. I remember thinking: *what bloody planet are you on?* Trying to return to planet Earth, I brought up the subject of Jason coming in to see him, and in an almost carefree way, John said the weekend would be fine.

When the meeting took place, it was not the emotion-charged, fairytale moment you would imagine. I was very disappointed in John. He was quiet but friendly towards Jason, and it was clear to see he had other things on his mind. I did not expect it to be easy, and thought with time John and Jason would have a chance to develop their relationship. After all, they had six years to catch up on. John had only seen his son twice before; once as a baby and three years later during the prison visit.

We knew it was going to take a long time for John to adjust to seeing his son, which is why we had spoken in depth about myself and Richard and my parents taking full responsibility for Jason. After nearly seven years in prison John had a lot of issues to sort out and he needed time for that. But he didn't even give his son a hug. I came away questioning if I had done the right thing in bringing Jason to Australia. *Did John even want him?* There was something strange in John's behaviour; he had become quite distant all of a sudden, and it worried me.

I kept bringing Jason in to see him in prison though. What else could I do? He was still phoning the house every day, but I can't remember him even once showing any interest in his son. He never asked about his schooling, his health or his general well-being, acting almost as if Jason didn't exist. Instead, the conversation would always lead elsewhere. He obviously had other things on his mind, but I didn't want to tackle him about this.

All of a sudden, I felt that I, and the rest of the family, were walking on eggshells around John, not wanting to upset or confront him in any way over his odd behaviour. I was more than happy he had started to make friends again, and was no longer reliant on me to do everything for him, or to be his only contact with the outside world. I wanted him to form normal relationships with other people, but more than anything, I wanted him to be a good father to Jason.

* * *

With school holidays coming to a close, I was more than looking forward to getting the boys back to school. I became a full-time Mum for the first time in ages, which was just what the boys needed after their mother's crusade to bring their uncle John back home and the many trips to Thailand it involved.

Jason was enrolled into Koondoola primary school where they have a wonderful intensive English language section. We felt he needed the intensive English language training an ordinary school could not provide. This meant a one-hour round trip in the morning and afternoon, so as well as getting the other three boys to school, working would have been impossible anyway.

It was very hard for Jason over the first month or so. Full-time school in a strange environment was proving to be a huge challenge for him. He was starting to pick up English at a great pace but refused to demonstrate this to his wonderful teacher Mrs Mobius. At one time she called in a Thai translator to speak to him, but he responded with stony silence and the odd tongue pulling. I could have crawled under a stone.

Jason loved playing the silent game, but on the way home from school he never stopped chatting and singing in broken English in the car. It was clear this child would try the patience of a saint, as my mother would say.

It was lovely to see Jason with Mum and Dad. Even up to a few months before, they would never in their wildest dreams have believed their youngest grandson would be sitting, drinking hot chocolate and having egg and chips at their kitchen table. Mum spending time reading to Jason was a sight to behold.

From being passed from pillar to post in Thailand, he was now surrounded by grandparents, aunts, uncles, and cousins who loved him dearly. Now, he also has all the opportunities our kids have. All that seemed to be missing was the love of his father.

* * *

When I next spoke with John he was very quiet and dragging out a conversation was hard work. Mum had the same experience. I was finding it very hard to cope with all of this and get my head around what had gone wrong, but one thing was clear; he was using us. In phoning us, he was going through the motions of keeping in touch. Richard and I had agreed to John living with us on his release, and we had also organised a job for him. These conditions were necessary for his early work release to be granted some time in March 2004. He knew he would burn his bridges if he cut off contact with us. Going through the motions of this hurt me no end, and just thinking that he was using me after all we'd been through was devastating. Six months earlier, he had told me his friend Paula had offered that he could live in her house when he was free, and as the pieces of the story fitted together the penny dropped that this was the plan and I was a mere stepping stone. He was able to erase the past six years, everything we had sacrificed for him, and simply move on.

Words can't describe how hurt I felt. I was absolutely devastated, angry and upset. *How could he do this?* Trying to keep my emotions in check was very hard, as I knew by his latest actions that he either knew his release date or was close to knowing. John called on a Saturday afternoon with the same old evasive conversation, but I was at my wit's end and decided to get it out in the open. I took a deep breath, and with knees trembling I said to him, 'I know what you are up to.' He played the innocent, and asked me what I was talking about. I reeled off everything I'd kept inside for weeks and told him he was not using Richard, the family and me anymore. I went on to tell him he'd better stick to his plan, which I knew in my heart was set for a day or so after he was released. I was in shock, and I couldn't believe the way John was acting, but it just kept getting worse.

I asked him if he was getting out very soon, but he gave no answer, so I asked if Paula was going to pick him up. His answer was one word: 'Yes.'

That was the biggest kick in the teeth he could have inflicted on us, after all we had been through to get him back to Australia. Not to mention the numerous heart wrenching trips to see him in Bangkok. I felt like someone had twisted a knife into my heart, it hurt so much. It was like an act of betrayal worse than anything I could imagine. *Did he know what he was doing to me? And to his family? Did he care?*

We had served our purpose and were no longer of any use to him, so he was casting us aside like trash. It would have meant so much to me to be there to see him walk out of prison a free man. All I wanted was to be there. Now, that was impossible.

After six years of pain, worry, fear, sacrifice, financial ruin, stress, the near-collapse of my family and my marriage, the search for Jason and taking him in, it had come to this. I shouted down the phone at him, 'After all we have done to get you back to Australia! Do you understand you would still be in Klong Prem prison for another two years if it wasn't for what we did?' I had never said that to him before; had never pointed out the suffering I had endured to get him out of that hellhole in Thailand, and I knew I was getting too emotional. His stone cold response was to ask, 'What did you do?' These words completely knocked me over, my head reeling and my mouth open in stunned disbelief, but after what seemed an eternity of silence, I suddenly burst into a tirade. 'What did you think all those trips to Thailand were for?' I asked, before listing everything we had done and everything we had sacrificed for him. But what came out of his mouth next was the killer blow.

He said that rather than making the seven trips to see him in prison, it would have been better if I had sent him AU$50 a month. That was it. That was the end. I put the phone down, completely numb, with his words ringing in my ears. *Who was this person to whom I'd just spoken? What had he turned into?* I couldn't comprehend what had just taken place, and swore that I would never speak to him again.

Over the next few days I was inconsolable. I just wanted to be alone to argue with myself, to trawl through the last years and wonder if I had in fact done the wrong thing in getting John back to Australia, fighting the government for three years to achieve something I thought was the most important thing in the world—the safety of my family. *Was I wrong to help John? Was I wrong to bring Jason to Australia? What had I done?*

* * *

I met up with my good friend Kath Mallott, who had been Head of the Aboriginal Deaths in Custody Watch Committee, and I knew she would be able to make some sense of the situation because of her involvement over many years with people who have been incarcerated and subsequently been engulfed by dysfunctional situations when released. We sat down for lunch, and without taking a breath, I poured my soul out. One thing she picked up on straight away was that if John had had his parole meeting the previous day, he would almost certainly be released the following day, which was that very day.

It turned out she was right. John was released that day. To think he was free, and hadn't even tried to call me, was hard to swallow, but he had made his choice and we will live with that, as will he, for years to come.

All I could think was that John must have been suffering from some sort of post-traumatic stress disorder that made him blind to what he was doing and the pain he was causing us. It was the only explanation I could find.

When I returned home from lunch, I rang Mum to tell her that I thought John might be out of prison. She was shocked but not altogether surprised, and immediately called the prison to find out. She was told he was not at the prison, but that was all the information that they could release. Because John was a high profile case and Mum and I went to the prison every week, we were familiar faces and everyone knew us well. Mum said the officer on the phone was sympathetic, and was no doubt scratching his head at the fact that John's own mother was not aware he'd been released.

I felt so sorry for Mum and Dad, and what made it worse for them was they had a house full of relatives, as many family members had come over from Liverpool to celebrate their fiftieth wedding anniversary. I wondered how on earth John could have been so selfish to put everyone through this.

Later that evening, my mother received a call from John. He was at his friend Paula's house, only three kilometres down the road. He was oblivious to the hurt he had caused, and even said he might pop in later. His blitheness and insensitivity cut deep; when Mum asked him why he hadn't let the family know that he was being released, he simply had nothing to say. Mum went on to tell him that he had hurt a lot of people, all of whom had been numbed and devastated by his actions, and not to act like he had done nothing wrong. No voices were raised and doors were left open to John, but it was clear he would have many bridges to mend. She didn't want to ban him from showing his face, but she did point out that the choices he had made to turn his back on his family would be something he had to live with. He made no mention of Jason, so it was clear he had no intentions of building a future with his son.

Over the next month or so, he made no attempt to see any of us, and the one comfort I had was that Jason was blissfully unaware of what had unfolded over the past few months, and was coming along amazingly well.

* * *

A few weeks later, when I got back from the school run, I decided to call Fiona, John's probation officer. I was worried about him because my son's friend Adam had met him and told us he was acting very strangely. Apparently he didn't respond at all when spoken to, as if Adam hadn't been there. What Fiona told me next was a complete shock. John was no longer under her supervision, because he had been granted a King's Royal Pardon four weeks previously. I was lost for words.

It had taken me nearly three years to prepare John's Pardon application, moving things along and putting as much effort into it as I did into the campaign to get the Prisoner Exchange Treaty ratified. And to think he never even had the decency to let me know he had been granted the Pardon—it just made me sick. This had to be the biggest stab in the heart.

Fiona went on to say she too was worried about John. I asked myself why he decided to abandon his family, who had worked so tirelessly to have him brought back to Australia? *Why else would he abandon his son?* With Fiona's news, the alarm bells started to ring in my head.

I was shaking with emotion and disbelief again, and wondered if John would ever cease to amaze me with his downright selfish behaviour and total lack of respect or concern for his family. It could almost have been understandable if we had become estranged, but I had literally crossed oceans and time zones to be with him when he needed me most, and the entire family had sacrificed so much without ever asking anything in return. All we wanted was to be there when he finally walked free, and to have John back. But he had come out of prison a different person. This wasn't John. I was completely dismayed at the thoughts of what he must have gone through to make him like this.

I called Mum and told her about the Pardon, and then dialled John's number. I had promised myself I would never speak to him again, but I wanted to give it one last try. Maybe he could change, become the old John, once he settled into life on the outside. Maybe his behaviour was down to what he went through.

'Hello, John speaking,' he said clearly.

I asked him if it was true he had been granted a King's Pardon.

He said yes.

My voice was breaking up; he was so cold.

I asked him why he did not tell us, but he just asked, 'Why would you want to know?'

At this point I raised my voice and told him it had taken me three years to organise, campaign for and submit that Pardon application, and asked did he honestly think I didn't want to know.

I was met with silence, so I asked him what bloody planet he was on. I was losing my cool, but he was ice cold, and calmly said, 'This one.'

He went on to say we had shunned him because he wanted his friend Paula to pick him up from prison when he was released.

One thing I will always remember from that conversation, if you could call it a conversation, was his total lack of emotion, and I can honestly say this was the brother I never knew. I vowed that I would never make excuses for him again. I always felt he was a very troubled but misunderstood person, but I now realise I was the one who misunderstood.

Over the next few hours I cried on and off. I was home alone, which was a blessing. I called Warren at the Australian Embassy in Bangkok, then the staff in Canberra. I wanted them to confirm the news, but I had been dealing with these people over the last few years and I guess I also needed them to know how things had turned out with John. Like everybody else who knows the story, they were shocked.

I felt so hurt; the knife continued to twist in my heart over the next few days, and the questions kept resurfacing in my mind: how could he do this to the people who devoted six years of their lives to him? No matter how many times I asked myself, it would never make sense. And it never will.

— CHAPTER TWELVE—

Moving on from the past few months of trauma was hard, but thank God I never had a minute to dwell on things. I now had four growing boys living in a three-bedroom house, and with little living area, this was proving difficult. We all needed space, so Richard and I decided it was best for the family if we moved house again.

I had finally started work again, so our financial situation was looking up, and the best option, we thought, was to build a house. We also found it great therapy, having an 'out with the old and in with the new' philosophy. We settled for the first house design we saw, got mortgaged up to the eyeballs, and bought a plot of land, moving into rented accommodation for the next 15 months. Jason was still attending a special English language school miles away, but we had no option as we wanted the best for him.

When I could grab some time, I would correspond with the inmates I'd now come to know as friends back in Bangkok, and it was not long before the Klong Prem Marathon Fundraiser 2004 was being planned. Before I knew it, I was back at work, campaigning for the prisoners and despite my disappointment of late, regarding John, I was enjoying it. It gave me a purpose, a chance to help those who needed it most, to raise money for Sister Joan's cause in the Bangkok slums and to raise the profiles of foreign inmates seeking a transfer home or a Pardon from the Thai King.

I was approached by ABC TV to feature our story on their award winning *Australian Story* documentary programme. Although it was an exciting thought, I felt anxious about dragging up the past, but after talking to the family we thought it might help us move on, while also generating some positive publicity for Sister Joan Evans' work in Bangkok.

We had just completed a fundraising drive in Perth for Sister Joan, and as usual my garage was brimming with donations for her and boxes of books for the prison. Now all I had to do was get them over to Thailand. I felt in my heart I needed this trip to Bangkok to tie up loose ends, but lots of people thought I was mad for returning. The way I saw it, when you are on a journey you have to see it through.

Plans were made and, again, without Mandy from Thai Airways I would never have got off the ground, literally. She organised a heavily discounted ticket, plus 60kg extra baggage allowance for the prison books and Sister Joan's donations. I'd arranged to do some filming in Bangkok with *ABC* but they would not be contributing to my trip financially, so once again I was on the phone to the manager at the Sofitel hotel who had always been so good to me. Without hesitation, he offered me a great deal, so everything was falling into place.

This trip was going to be chaotic, not unlike the previous nine, but in a very different way. It was a strange feeling knowing John was back in Australia and estranged from our family, and when I went to see Trevor at Klong Prem the next day, I felt as if John's ghost was present. I could almost see him walking through that door, and found myself squinting to get a clear view of him through the micromesh in the 'chook pen' visiting area.

While waiting for Trevor to come through, I was overcome with sadness and disbelief as I took in the sights I had become so familiar with. I let out a deep sigh, and felt myself about to break down in tears, but right on cue, there was Trevor bounding his way into the visit area. 'Mrs Singh!' he called, in his very proper English accent, and I instantly snapped out of it. Once again he had saved me from emotional meltdown, but he didn't even know it.

Trevor had my work cut out for the next few days. I was to phone and e-mail the hierarchy at the Prison Corrections Department, hoping they would allow the media and myself attend the marathon to be run inside the prison the following Sunday.

After the visit, I made my way to the prison shop to buy food for Trevor and a few other inmates I had gotten to know. At this stage I knew exactly what to buy. They loved the special treats like fresh fruit and coffee, not to mention cigarettes and toiletries. My friends Sue and Elizabeth, who spend a lot of time in Bangkok and visit Trevor and other inmates, fondly call the food shopping 'The Harvest Festival'.

The previous marathon in 2003 had gone like clockwork, but true to form, all the rules had changed and it was becoming painfully clear the decision makers did not want to know. We received support from some officials but in the end their help came to nothing and it looked like nothing was going to happen. Trevor and I became angry and frustrated, having spent a long time trying to organise everything. Trevor in particular sharply felt the disappointment at our lack of progress. He had spent months training and organising everything from the most difficult place imaginable; behind the bars of the Bangkok Hilton, but he persevered. He had assembled a fine team of runners from all over the world, making sure the marathon was represented by inmates from Africa, Europe and Asia.

We decided it would be best if I just turned up on the day of the planned marathon, hoping for the best. Trevor felt I had a knack of bringing miracles with me. We did at least plan to have an auction again, and my cousin Sean had managed to get a football signed by the Liverpool team, so that would bring in some much-needed funds for Sister Joan.

I was still filming with *ABC*, and after days of hectic planning, I was desperate for an early night, having to get to Klong Prem by 6am for the marathon. I set off on the familiar journey to the prison, not feeling the excitement I'd felt twelve months earlier. As we approached the front gate, all I could see was a pack of half a dozen flea-bitten dogs sleeping off the day before, not even flinching as my taxi pulled up inches from them.

I was tempted to ask the driver to wait, but quickly thought of all the other miracles that had come out of the blue. Walking through the gate was a stark contrast to last year. There was no media, no celebratory red white and blue Thai flags; just two yawning guards waiting for their shift to finish. They were bemused to see this *farang* woman asking them, in my best pidgin Thai, 'Is the Marathon on?'

'No, not today,' they said, 'it's finished… gone.'

I knew there was no point in hanging around so I headed back to the hotel and called Yvonne to let her know the bad news. I just hoped they allowed the boys to run so that it was not a total white wash for them. I could not wait for the next day to come so I could go to see Trevor and find out what went wrong.

The next morning at Klong Prem I was approached by the foreign affairs guard apologising for the confusion of the past few days, which was a nice gesture. Yvonne and I made our way through to the visit area and after a few minutes Trevor appeared. I did not have to look twice to see he was very upset, and I couldn't get the words out quick enough.

'What went on?' I asked. He explained that some official had pulled the plug on the marathon being run through the main prison grounds, but allowed them to run in the courtyard of their building. Trevor and the guys did not give up, and made the most of the situation, completing the 42kms faster than the previous year and going on to raise thousands of dollars for Sister Joan. It was not the success of the previous year, but it was still a success. Sister Joan would get much-needed funds, the inmates' profiles had been raised, and they had, for a few months, been given something to work towards, adding meaning to their lives. To me, every minute was more than worthwhile, and the whole campaign, with the determination of Trevor and the other inmates to do this for a deserving charity that helped the poorest of the poor, helped to restore my faith in humanity after it had suffered a near-fatal blow.

* * *

Jason has now settled into Australian life remarkably well. His English is amazing and he is doing very well at school. He has a weekly sleepover at Nana and Granddad's, and I can truly say there is never a dull moment in our household. John has only once visited Jason in two years, even though he lives less than three kilometres away, and nobody in my family, including Mum and Dad, hears from him.

Richard and I consider Jason our son now; he calls Richard Dad and me Mum, and he's quite simply a part of our family. And he will be forever. The door will never be closed for John to walk back into our lives, because he will always be Jason's father, my brother and my parents' son, but he has to change for that to happen. I prefer not to focus on the past anymore; I prefer to look to the future.

Our priority now is this beautiful little boy called Jason who is the centre of our family's world. Watching him grow makes all the sacrifices we made, and all the heartache my family and I suffered, more than worth it.

— AFTERWORD —

This is the tale of a woman whose loyalty and determination brought about changes in her life she could never even have dreamed of. Where others would have been bitter and defeated, Debbie Singh went on to bigger and better things in an ongoing quest to help others who have little or no support.

I first became aware of Debbie when she used to visit her brother in Klong Prem Prison, at which time I was the prison visitor on behalf of the Australian Embassy in Bangkok. However, I only came face-to-face with her for the first time when Sister Joan Evans, a Catholic sister doing charity work in the Klong Toey slums, invited me to meet her friend from Perth who was staying near Bangkok Airport. And there was Debbie! Surrounded by food for John, donated clothes for Sister Joan's slum children, and the results of shopping excursions for clothes and treats to take back to her beloved sons in Perth. Debbie never does one thing at a time!

From that time on I was in touch with Debbie, at times on a daily basis, as she worked through the endless red tape of the Prisoner Transfer Treaty, and later with identifying the needs of other prisoners in the harsh conditions of the Thai Prisons. The list of her activities in support of others in need does not end there, but includes assisting foreign prisoners in Australian jails, fundraising efforts for Sister Joan, and the charity marathon run organised by a British prisoner, Trevor Lund. Debbie never slows down and the standing joke is that one of these days we will actually get to have a cold beer together!

Twice, to my knowledge, Debbie has had the wind knocked out of her sails. Once when she failed to see what her relentless pursuit of justice was doing to her family life, and secondly when John was quietly released from prison to freedom and another life. Each time she has taken stock, set a new course, and, as you will have read, has gone on to achieve more and more.

Debbie has proved that ordinary people can achieve extraordinary things, but with true humility, she is surprised that people find her story worth telling.

Here's to you, Debbie. Thank you for sharing, caring and actually doing something for other people.

Yvonne Ziegler, Official Prison Visits Officer, Australian Embassy, Bangkok